The Woman is the Glory of the Man

(The Curse of the Creation in Eden)

George Davis

WestBow Press books may be ordered through booksellers or by contacting:

WestBow Press
A Division of Thomas Nelson
1663 Liberty Drive
Bloomington, IN 47403
www.westbowpress.com
1-(866) 928-1240

ISBN: 978-1-4497-5748-9 (sc)
ISBN: 978-1-4497-5749-6 (hc)
ISBN: 978-1-4497-5747-2 (e)

Library of Congress Control Number: 2012911371

Printed in the United States of America

WestBow Press rev. date: 07/10/2012

Contents

Acknowledgments

I would like to give all credit to the Holy Spirit who without His guidance I would have never come to the understanding of the Spiritual relationships and responsibilities given out to the man and the woman. The Bible states that the things of God are "Spiritually discerned." He allowed me to observe this spiritual realm from different perspectives, all the time keeping His hand firmly on me. Thus, when I was ready to be used of Him, I could spiritually understand the "things" He taught. I am in awe of what He showed me.

INTRODUCTION

The Catholic Church tells me I'm headed to Hell because I disagree with their teaching of Purgatory, do not consider the Pope the *Holy Father*, and refuse to pray to any of their saints. The Jehovah's Witnesses claim that God has given me up to a disapproved mental state, to do the things not fitting because I believe in the doctrine of the *Trinity*. Many Lutheran churches will not allow me to share *Communion* with them because the pastor must first approve my Christian walk according to their statement of faith. A Baptist Church did not allow me to share the 'A-millennial' point of view with the congregation because they believe in 'pre-millennial' Doctrine. And when mentioning that a woman should be silent in the church, the Watchman Nee group I was attending was very, very upset with me.

The Bible brings God's Truth to this world. It claims this. Along with millions of Christians throughout history, I believe the Bible's claims to be true. What I do not believe is many of the doctrines and teachings that come out of these *Houses of God*. Many things they teach are devoid of spiritual understanding and application. The Bible teaches *Spiritually* first and foremost. This is because we (mankind) are created spiritually first and foremost. We are commanded to worship our Creator in our spirit.

John 4:23 "But the hour cometh, and now is, when the true worshippers shall worship the Father in spirit and in truth: for the Father seeketh such to worship him."

This verse in John teaches us that the true worshippers will worship God both in spirit and in truth. How does one worship the Father in this manner? To answer this we must first come to an understanding of what the word 'spirit' means. For most of us, we must rely on someone who has studied the language being used and thus has produced some form of interpretation for the public. Laymen then can utilize these *works* for guidance in their study. One of these self-helps is called a concordance. It takes a Hebrew, Aramaic, or Greek word in Scripture and translates this word into English. It also shows us where this word is used all throughout the Bible. This will give the student a chance to compare scripture with scripture giving them a clearer understanding of its use in any context given. I have chosen the Strong's exhaustive concordance of the Bible for this purpose. It is based on the Kings James version of the Bible (which are the Scripture verses you see used). In John 4:23 the word spirit is mainly identified as a current of air or a breath. Figuratively it means a spirit or the soul. For the intention of sharing spiritual concepts to the reader, any definition I use will be taken from the Strong's concordance and will be displayed on the page in this manner.

Spirit #4151 a current of air, i.e. breath (blast) or a breeze; by anal. or fig. a spirit, i.e. (human) the rational soul, (by impl.) vital principle, ment. Disposition, etc., (superhuman) an angel, demon, or (divine) God, Christ's spirit, the Holy Spirit [from 4154 a primary word; to breathe hard, i.e. breeze]

We see immediately that just to know the translation of the word 'spirit' (a current of air) will not be enough to help us make a conclusion. We will need to have more information.

Job 32:8 "But there is a spirit in man: and the inspiration of the Almighty giveth them understanding."

This teaches that any deep understanding must be given (or inspired) from God. We simply cannot reason this out on our own.

1 Corinthians 2:10-12 "But God hath revealed them unto us by his Spirit: for the Spirit searcheth all things, yea, the deep things of God. For what man knoweth the things of a man, save the spirit of man which is in him? even so the things of God knoweth no man, but the Spirit of God. Now we have received, not the spirit of the world, but the spirit which is of God; that we might know the things that are freely given to us of God."

When God has given us His understanding, only then can one worship Him in Spirit and in truth. This is why the unsaved cannot worship God in a way that is pleasing to Him.

1 Corinthians 2:14 "But the natural man receiveth not the things of the Spirit of God: for they are foolishness unto him: neither can he know them, because they are spiritually discerned."

So just knowing the meaning of the word in a sentence isn't enough. We need something more. We need spiritual instruction from above. Note that students that study Hebrew, Aramaic, or

Greek may spend many years trying to understand how each word is to be interpreted and how it is applied in the context given. This should mean a master linguist should be able to unlock the deep hidden mysteries of Scripture just by knowledge of the language. But this isn't the case. The Bible is parabolic and speaks through symbols and in allegories. This type of understanding requires help from God's Spirit, giving us a spiritual understanding. Unfortunately, the churches and congregations of today no longer teach how to understand Scripture spiritually.

1 Thessalonians 5:23 "And the very God of peace sanctify you wholly; and I pray God your whole spirit and soul and body be preserved blameless unto the coming of our Lord Jesus Christ."

We are a creation composed of a body, a soul, and a spirit. In the churches we are taught about our body and to some extent our soul. But what do we know about our spirit? It is extremely imperative to address this issue because it is where we receive knowledge from God, and where we spiritually discern this information. But most significantly, it is the portion where the Holy Spirit indwells us.

Romans 8:16 "The Spirit itself beareth witness with our spirit, that we are the children of God:"

This is Spirit to spirit communication. He is in us. Separate from our soul and our flesh. The frightening aspect of this is that this spirit of ours will allow other *spirits* to indwell us. We can see this displayed from Old Testament and New Testament passages.

1 Samuel 16:14 "But the Spirit of the LORD departed from Saul, and an evil spirit from the LORD troubled him."

Luke 11:24-26 "When the unclean spirit is gone out of a man, he walketh through dry places, seeking rest; and finding none, he saith, I will return unto my house whence I came out. And when he cometh, he findeth it swept and garnished. Then goeth he, and taketh to him seven other spirits more wicked than himself; and they enter in, and dwell there: and the last state of that man is worse than the first."

This unclean spirit (as does the Holy Spirit) can dwell in this part of us. Note that our spirit is referred to as a house. It is also the place that channels an entity or spiritually gives a reading through some New Age method. It is used in *speaking of tongues* and the following interpretation of them. When *slain* in the Spirit we are dealing with that portion of us. And when used of God to bring *prophesy* to others, our spirit is part of that process.

2 Samuel 23:2 "The Spirit of the LORD spake by me, and his word was in my tongue."

When our soul is saved this spirit receives an Eternal connection to the Holy Spirit. This is the way we live in Him and He lives in us. Our soul will then live forever. If one is not saved, this Spirit returns to Him (the Creator) who gave it and that soul dies.

Ecclesiastes 12:7 "Then shall the dust return to the earth as it was: and the spirit shall return unto God who gave it."

Body and Soul can be destroyed, but the Spirit that is given to us is not. That is because God will not kill His own Spirit. "But the soul that sinneth, it shall die."

Matthew 10:28 "And fear not them which kill the body, but are not able to kill the soul: but rather fear him which is able to destroy both soul and body in hell."

Note that this verse does not include the spirit being destroyed. Needless to say, coming to an understanding of this spirit part of us is very important. And this issue becomes more complicated when we add in the spiritual headship that God gave to the man and the woman to follow.

1 Corinthians 11:3 "But I would have you know, that the head of every man is Christ; and the head of the woman is the man; and the head of Christ is God."

What concept do you think God is teaching here? Lets look at this as a spiritual authority He is commanding us to follow. We read that God is the head of Christ. Jesus prayed to the Father for strength, and was obedient to every law commanded. Even dying on the cross for Him "nevertheless not my will, but thine, be done". He did everything that God asked of Him. Pastors and Priests will teach this boldly to their congregations. And they do the same with "the head of every man is Christ." After all, doesn't the man pray to Him for strength, and to save him? And is to obey the law of Christ? (Gal 6:2) Most do not have a problem discerning what this verse is teaching. But then we come to "the head of the woman is the man." Are we not to apply these words as we apply God to Christ, Christ to man? Churches do not, in fact, they teach the exact opposite. "The man and the woman are equals in the congregation," they say, "God is not a respecter of persons."

1 Corinthians 14:34-35 "Let your women keep silence in the churches: for it is not permitted unto them to speak; but they are commanded to be under obedience, as also saith the law. And if they will learn any thing, let them ask their husbands at home: for it is a shame for women to speak in the church."

When we read in the Bible "let your women keep silent in the churches", do we really understand what God is commanding here? Most pastors, priests, and teachers make a weak attempt explaining what this means in their sermons. They avoid confrontational truths, and instead try to joke their way around them. I have listened to many different pastoral doctrines as to what this is really teaching, but the real discernment of this is lost, especially the Spiritual understanding of these verses. This style of worship was practiced in the days of the Old Testament. Jesus participated in this Temple worship and found no problem with this "women keep silent" percept.

1 Corinthians 11:7-10 "For a man indeed ought not to cover his head, forasmuch as he is the image and glory of God: but the woman is the glory of the man. For the man is not of the woman; but the woman of the man. Neither was the man created for the woman; but the woman for the man. For this cause ought the woman to have power on her head because of the angels."

The man is the head of the woman. He is the spiritual leader, the spiritual *covering* for the one flesh. But today in most relationships, it is the woman who is the spiritual leader. She will drag the husband or boyfriend into a church or a Bible study. In the marriage it is commanded that the man is to be the head of the woman (the spiritual head), but now the woman is either the equal to him (two spiritual heads), or she is *the* (spiritual) head of the man. That is in rebellion to God's Word. And it conflicts with our direct communication (prayers) to Him. We are hindering that process and approaching the Father incorrectly.

Much of what is taught today from Scripture lacks true spiritual understanding. We are taught to be spiritually ignorant. It is in this way that the Holy Spirit is quenched from our lives. And the Holy Spirit is our only true Spiritual teacher.

Matthew 24:44-47 "Therefore be ye also ready: for in such an hour as ye think not the Son of man cometh. Who then is a faithful and wise servant, whom his lord hath made ruler over his household, to give them meat in due season? Blessed is that servant, whom his lord when he cometh shall find so doing. Verily I say unto you, That he shall make him ruler over all his goods."

In a marriage, it is the man that is to *rule* over his household. This is a spiritual *rule* first and foremost. And when we apply this spiritual understanding to those *cultural sexist* passages demeaning women in Scripture, it is clear to us that that is a wrong assumption.

Genesis 3:16 "Unto the woman he said, I will greatly multiply thy sorrow and thy conception; in sorrow thou shalt bring forth children; and thy desire shall be to thy husband, and he shall rule over thee."

This verse in Genesis when *Spiritually* understood explains why God wrote in the New Testament to the churches about the behavior of the women there. It explains why the women must be silent in the churches. It explains why if they will learn anything; let them ask their husbands at home, and it explains why the wife is the weaker vessel.

Unfortunately today both the man and woman are in rebellion to the curses that were given out in the Garden of Eden. Satan has been very successful in attacking this 'Planned Godhood' program. This is why Divorce is so prevalent in our day. Separate the husband and wife. Remove the spiritual covering of the marriage, and turn them away from the blessings of God by blaspheming the Word.

Titus 2:5 "To be discreet, chaste, keepers at home, good, obedient to their own husbands, that the word of God be not blasphemed."

We do not want the Word of God to be blasphemed. It's a good thing most women are obedient to their own husbands. What? Most women are not obedient to their husbands? Most husbands are obedient to their wives? This would be very funny except for the fact that this reversal of spiritual headship is one of the signs the Bible gives to us to indicate the return of Christ. One of the common denominators I have found in my travels through the churches and congregations (outside of "believe as us or perish in Hell") is that many in these groups believe that the return of Christ is near. And I believe this to be true also. With apologies to those who believe in the pre-millennial doctrine and are waiting for something to happen to Israel, the biggest warning of the end times is primarily focused on the marriage between the man and the woman. Remember, they will be marrying and giving in marriage just as in the days of Noah when Christ returns. Every time the woman becomes the spiritual head in the Bible, God brings that rule to an end.

Isaiah 3:12 "As for my people, children are their oppressors, and women rule over them. O my people, they which lead thee cause thee to err, and destroy the way of thy paths."

Women challenging men for the spiritual headship is taught all through the Scriptures. This is a pattern we are now following in the world. When this scenario happens in the Bible, God makes big changes for those involved shortly afterwards. This is imminent.

Isaiah 28:9-10 "Whom shall he teach knowledge? and whom shall he make to understand doctrine? them that are weaned from the milk, and drawn from the breasts. For precept must be upon precept, precept upon precept; line upon line, line upon line; here a little, and there a little:"

In the following chapters, I will show the reader from the Bible how God in His infinite Mercy, gives us examples of this doctrine of Spiritual headship and authority. Starting from the creation of the man and woman, and the spiritual curses that are with us even to today. We will read about the fall of the sons of God that brought on the flood of Noah's day, and King Solomon (who is a picture of the church), how he was eventually overcome by the women in his life. We will see why the man was given authority over a woman's vow to God and why this is still in effect today. Why a woman is bound to her husband as long as he lives and the reason she is called the weaker vessel. But most importantly, we will see how the marriage relationship in

Scripture has always been a sign to us of a coming judgment from God. When we look at our society today, and at the destruction of the marriage institution, it is a clear sign that the return of Christ and His final judgment of mankind is very near.

2 Timothy 3:16 "All scripture is given by inspiration of God, and is profitable for doctrine, for reproof, for correction, for instruction in righteousness:"

The Bible teaches us that it is the man who has the spiritual authority over the woman, and that the woman is to submit to his authority. We must return to this "instruction in righteousness" or face a severe judgment from our Creator.

Ezekiel 3:20-21 "Again, When a righteous man doth turn from his righteousness, and commit iniquity, and I lay a stumblingblock before him, he shall die: because thou hast not given him warning, he shall die in his sin, and his righteousness which he hath done shall not be remembered; but his blood will I require at thine hand. Nevertheless if thou warn the righteous man, that the righteous sin not, and he doth not sin, he shall surely live, because he is warned; also thou hast delivered thy soul."

The Creation Of Mankind

Genesis 1:26-27 "And God said, Let us make man in our image, after our likeness: and let them have dominion over the fish of the sea, and over the fowl of the air, and over the cattle, and over all the earth, and over every creeping thing that creepeth upon the earth. So God created man in his own image, in the image of God created he him; male and female created he them."

God is going to create something incredibly special, a representation of God Himself. A human man in His Godly Image. He will have dominion over fish, fowl, cattle, the earth, and all creeping things. Students of the Bible have been taught this is a literal, physical description of what is to come. And literally, it has come to pass. But unfortunately, the spiritual significance of what is taught here is almost non-existent. Throughout the Bible, God will use animals to describe groups of people. The most notable are sheep and goats. Individuals are identified in the same way. Jesus is represented as a lamb and Satan as a dragon. God uses these types of descriptions to teach us deeper spiritual meanings.

Isaiah 30:6 "The burden of the beasts of the south: into the land of trouble and anguish, from whence come the young and old lion, the viper and fiery flying serpent, they will carry their riches upon the shoulders of young asses, and their treasures upon the bunches of camels, to a people that shall not profit them."

Here in Isaiah, we see many *animals* used to describe various groups. It is very apparent in this verse that this is what is going on. But there are many passages in the Bible where it is not that obvious. The Creation account is full of these. The first chapter of Genesis teaches not only the creation of the earth and the heavens, but also the creation of the Salvation plan of God. This is spiritually illustrated through the *light* God creates and then divides. Now these plants and animals described here in Chapter one are also referred to throughout Scripture-words like herb, tree, fish, fowl, cattle, and beast. These classifications of *living things* have deep spiritual meanings. A further study of these would help us come to understand God's Salvation plan in a more informative way.

In Genesis One they also have deep spiritual meanings. But here we will focus on the man and woman's creation.

Genesis 1:26 "And God said, Let us make man in our image, after our likeness: and let them have dominion over the fish of the sea, and over the fowl of the air, and over the cattle, and over all the earth, and over every creeping thing that creepeth upon the earth."

"Let us make man in our image, after our likeness." First, the Temple of God needs a shepherd. Someone who can reflect the

'Will of God.' This will be the *man* made in the image of God. So we first need to understand what this *image* is.

Image #6754 from an unused root meaning to shade, a phantom, i.e. (fig) illusion, resemblance; hence, a representative

To understand its true meaning, we will need to compare scripture with scripture.

Romans 8:29-30 "For whom he did foreknow, he also did predestinate to be conformed to the image of his Son, that he might be the firstborn among many brethren. Moreover whom he did predestinate, them he also called: and whom he called, them he also justified: and whom he justified, them he also glorified."

We read that the predestinated are conformed to an image of his Son (Jesus Christ).

2 Corinthians 4:4 "In whom the god of this world hath blinded the minds of them which believe not, lest the light of the glorious gospel of Christ, who is the image of God, should shine unto them."

This image reflects the *light* of the Gospel of Christ who is the image of God.

Colossians 1:15 "Who is the image of the invisible God, the firstborn of every creature:"

This image is Jesus Christ who is the firstborn of every creature.

Colossians 3:10-12 "And have put on the new man, which is renewed in knowledge after the image of him that created him: Where there is neither Greek nor Jew, circumcision nor uncircumcision, Barbarian, Scythian, bond nor free: but Christ is all, and in all. Put on therefore, as the elect of God, holy and beloved, bowels of mercies, kindness, humbleness of mind, meekness, longsuffering;"

This renewed in knowledge reflects the image of God. It is given to the elect of God.

It is a *spiritual state* of being or existing. This image represents the Creator on Earth. Note that this part of creation is spiritual. God would begin his *man* with that because:

John 4:24 "God is a Spirit: and they that worship him must worship him in spirit and in truth."

These elect of God are chosen before the foundation of the World. This is the light that is created in Genesis 1:3. They receive this *image* from Him in order to do His Will.

Before we look at the likeness of God, we should see how the Bible describes man.

Man #120 ruddy, i.e. human being (an individual or the species, mankind, etc...) [from 119 to show blood (in the face) i.e. flush or turn rosy]

Ruddy is a reddish like color, the kind that appears on your cheeks if your face begins to flush or turn rosy. Ruddy is a color identified with mankind. It is our blood that produces this reddish color. It would be safe to say that blood and the color of it identifies us.

Leviticus 17:11 "For the life of the flesh is in the blood: and I have given it to you upon the altar to make an atonement for your souls: for it is the blood that maketh an atonement for the soul."

Deuteronomy 12:23 "Only be sure that thou eat not the blood: for the blood is the life; and thou mayest not eat the life with the flesh."

Psalm 94:21 "They gather themselves together against the soul of the righteous, and condemn the innocent blood."

Genesis 4:10b "...the voice of thy brother's blood crieth unto me from the ground."

"Let us make 'ruddy' in our Image..." Man is identified in these passages with blood.

Blood is the life. Blood can "maketh an atonement for the soul". Blood cries out to God.

Man is, in a sense, a plasma bag filled with (type *you* blood.) Is this what God means when he says "in the likeness"? Blood as we see it or feel it? What is this "likeness"?

Likeness #1823 resemblance; model; shape; adverbially like [from 1819 PR to compare; by implication to resemble, liken, consider]

To understand this likeness, lets see how man was originally created.

Genesis 2:7 "And the LORD God formed man of the dust of the ground, and breathed into his nostrils the breath of life; and man became a living soul."

The "likeness of God" isn't the dust or the flesh. It is the living soul. The *Life*. God is the Tree of Life. He has the Book of Life. Made after our likeness means to have independent life from God. This life is placed in the Blood. And God's Spirit keeps this life alive.

Job 33:4 "The Spirit of God hath made me, and the breath of the Almighty hath given me life."

The Spirit of God is my image, and the breath of Almighty God is my likeness to him.

In Genesis chapter 5, we see the likeness and image passed on from a human to a human.

Genesis 5:3 "And Adam lived an hundred and thirty years, and begat a son in his own likeness, after his image; and called his name Seth:"

Adam, through the miracle of birth begats a son or gives life to it. This is "in his own likeness." This follows the likeness of life given by God to Adam. The Bible does not use the word (likeness) in this fashion after this verse. The begats take over. Note that Adam begats a son after his image, Seth. (#8352 put, i.e. substituted) The Scripture clearly states his image. This of course had to happen. Humans now are involved with God's spiritual image. The original Image of God begins to change into something else. It changes into the spiritual image of man. We see this progression in Genesis chapter 4.

Genesis 4:26 "And to Seth, to him also there was born a son; and he called his name Enos: then began men to call upon the name of the LORD."

Notice that the absence of this *Image* brings men to "call upon the name of the LORD."

This image ties in perfectly with the *knowledge* of God in man slowly disappearing.

Genesis 1:27 "So God created man in his own image, in the image of God created he him; male and female created he them."

Created #1254 Primitive root (absolutely) to create; (qualified) to cut down (a wood), select, feed (as formative processes)

Image #6754 from an unused root meaning to shade, a phantom, i.e. (fig) illusion, resemblance; hence, a representative

Genesis 5:1-2 "This is the book of the generations of Adam. In the day that God created man, in the likeness of God made he him; Male and female created he them; and blessed them, and called their name Adam, in the day when they were created."

The man created in God's Image is Adam. "In the likeness of God made He him." This man who is God's representation on earth can now lead his congregation. This congregation will come from the body of Adam. But before we look at that, lets look at the work Adam did before the woman shows up. God plants a garden eastward in Eden in an environment that includes "every tree that is pleasant to the sight."

Genesis 2:15 "And the LORD God took the man, and put him into the garden of Eden to dress it and to keep it."

Dress #5647 to work (in any sense), by implication to serve, till, (causative) enslave

Keep #8104 to hedge about (as with thorns), i.e. guard; (gen) to protect, attend to, etc.

Note that this man is an individual person and not referring to mankind here, although Adam spiritually represents men of God. Adam's job is to serve this garden. To protect or guard it. Guard it against what? Against the evil that is to come. [A test for Adam]

There are a couple of interesting points in Chapter 2. The first, which is the most important, is that God gives a commandment to Adam limiting him to what he can *eat*. He is not to eat of the tree of the knowledge of good and evil. This will bring death. The second, which is related to this, is that Adam eats from the trees. They are good for food. After Adam is cursed, he eats of the ground and of the herbs of the field.

Genesis 2:18 "And the LORD God said, It is not good that the man should be alone; I will make him an help meet for him."

Alone #905 separation; by implication a part of the body, branch of a tree, bar for carrying; figuratively chief of a city; especially as adverb, apart, only, besides

Help #5828 aid [from 5826 (a primitive root) to surround, i.e. protect or aid]

"It is not good that the man should be alone." Adam is separated from God in a sense. He is alone in that way. Adam also (as a man of God) has no congregation. He is a branch with no fruit. This is not good God declares. He will make Adam "an help meet."

Genesis 2:19-20 "And out of the ground the LORD God formed every beast of the field, and every fowl

of the air; and brought them unto Adam to see what he would call them: and whatsoever Adam called every living creature, that was the name thereof. And Adam gave names to all cattle, and to the fowl of the air, and to every beast of the field; but for Adam there was not found an help meet for him."

Name #8034 a primitive word; an appellation, as a mark or memorial of individuality; by implication honor, authority, character

Again, we will just concentrate on the study of the man and woman here rather than the spiritual meanings for the animals listed. Adam is given the task of naming every living creature. God names everybody in the Book of Life. What both of them name, it stays.

Adam has *dominion* over all of these animals. But still no help meet for him. Now many teachers suggest that Adam was depressed because he was alone. God saw this and decided to create a woman for him. This will make Adam happy in the Garden of Eden. But we do not read anywhere that Adam was wanting for anything.

Ephesians 1:4-5 "According as he hath chosen us in him before the foundation of the world, that we should be holy and without blame before him in love: Having predestinated us unto the adoption of children by Jesus Christ to himself, according to the good pleasure of his will,"

God hath *chosen us* in him before the foundation of the world. All these *predestinated* people have to be born. Therefore sin must enter into the Garden of Eden so God's Salvation plan can begin. God again mentions the absence of a helper for the man Adam.

Suited (for him) #5048 a front, i.e. part opposite; specifically a counterpart, or mate; usually (adverb especially with prep.) over against or before [from 5046 to front, i.e. stand boldly out opposite; by implication (causative), to manifest; (fig) to announce; specifically to expose...]

God will now create this help meet, this (opposite or counterpart) for the man.

Genesis 2:21-22 "And the LORD God caused a deep sleep to fall upon Adam, and he slept: and he took one of his ribs, and closed up the flesh instead thereof; And the rib, which the LORD God had taken from man, made he a woman, and brought her unto the man."

Sleep/Slept #3462 to be slack or languid, i.e. (by implication) sleep (fig) to die; also to grow old, state, or inveterate

Rib #6763 a rib (as curved), lit. (of the body) or fig. (of a door, i.e. leaf); hence, a side, lit. (of a person) or fig. (of an object or the sky, i.e. quarter); timber or plank (i.e. flooring)

There is an interesting fact that comes up when we see the creation of the woman.

Genesis 2:7 "And the LORD God formed man of the dust of the ground, and breathed into his nostrils the breath of life; and man became a living soul."

God forms the man from the dust of the ground. Adam is created.

Genesis 2:9 "And out of the ground made the LORD God to grow every tree that is pleasant to the sight, and good for food; the tree of life also in the midst of the garden, and the tree of knowledge of good and evil."

The trees and the plants are created out of the ground.

Genesis 2:19 ""And out of the ground the LORD God formed every beast of the field, and every fowl of the air; and brought them unto Adam to see what he would call them: and whatsoever Adam called every living creature, that was the name thereof."

Every beast of the field and every fowl of the air are formed from the ground. We see here that God uses the *ground* as a base substance for His creations. But with the woman, we have a different base substance. God creates her out of a rib from Adam.

Genesis 2:22 "And the rib, which the LORD God had taken from man, made he a woman, and brought her unto the man."

God makes the woman out of Adam's rib. The direct (make in the image and after our likeness) is done through the body of Adam. There is a difference in the "Image."

1 Corinthians 11:7-9 "For a man indeed ought not to cover his head, forasmuch as he is the image and glory of God: but the woman is the glory of the man. For the man is not of the woman; but the woman of the man. Neither was the man created for the woman; but the woman for the man."

"For the man is not of the woman, but the woman of the man." Our Creator tells us that there is an important difference between the man and the woman. (I know that we are all born the same way, this is a creation observation I am sharing.)

I would like to address the matter of the *rib*. I've heard many guesses as to what the rib represents in Scripture. Let's look at the meaning of the word rib.

Rib #6763 a rib (as curved), lit. (of the body) or fig. (of a door, i.e. leaf); hence, a side, lit. (of a person) or fig. (of an object or the sky, i.e. quarter); timber or plank (i.e. flooring)

In Genesis 1:27 and in 5:2, we read "Male and Female created he them."

Male #2145 Remembered, i.e. a male (of man or animals, as being the most noteworthy sex) [from 2142 a primitive root; to mark (so as to be recognized) i.e. to remember; by implication to mention; also to be male]

Female #5347 a female (from the sexual form) [from 5344 a primitive root, to puncture, (literally to perforate, with more or less violence) or fig. to specify, designate, libel]

People are surprised by the Bible's definition of the word *female*. God makes a clear distinction as to the importance between her and the male. And this is not just a reference to Eve. It represents all women throughout time. She is created from a rib (the emphasis on the shape), and is identified by her sexual form (female). In both, the *curve* of her form is the identifying mark, whereas for the male, the name itself is remembered or marked. This gives us a clue as to why there is a spiritual headship between the two.

This *shape* can also reflect the spiritual state of the gender. To be straight is to be on a path toward God. To be crooked (or curved), is to be on a path away from God.

Luke 3:5-6 "Every valley shall be filled, and every mountain and hill shall be brought low; and the crooked shall be made straight, and the rough ways shall be made smooth; And all flesh shall see the salvation of God."

Luke 13:13 "And he laid his hands on her: and immediately she was made straight, and glorified God."

2 Corinthians 6:11-12 "O ye Corinthians, our mouth is open unto you, our heart is enlarged. Ye are not straitened in us, but ye are straitened in your own bowels."

Here God uses shapes to convey the spiritual state of an individual in the Bible. I believe this is the spiritual meaning of rib. Could this be because she is not made in the image?

That would certainly make her more vulnerable to evil. She may even get *deceived.*

Most pastors teach that because the woman came out of the side of Adam, that they are equal. This is a very superficial way of looking at the creation of the man and the woman. With that as their foundation, their teachings on men and women will lead those that listen to them away from the truth. They will never understand the spiritual authority given to the male.

Genesis 2:23 "And Adam said, This is now bone of my bones, and flesh of my flesh: she shall be called Woman, because she was taken out of Man."

Adam continues his job of naming all the living creatures that God brings to him. He calls her woman because she is (of the man). We find that later he will change her name to Eve (because she will be the mother of all living.) "This is now bone of my bones, and flesh of my flesh." Adam is the original form and the woman is the copy. A creation that is made from him. Adam has dominion over the woman (his wife) because God wanted this system for mankind.

1 Corinthians 11:3 "But I would have you know, that the head of every man is Christ; and the head of the woman is the man; and the head of Christ is God."

This is the spiritual pecking order God has set up. The man is made in the Image of God. The Pastor (husband) has the headship over the congregation (his wife). This spiritual order should be found in every marriage. Every husband has been given the responsibility to spiritually lead his household.

Genesis 2:24-25 "Therefore shall a man leave his father and his mother, and shall cleave unto his wife: and they shall be one flesh. And they were both naked, the man and his wife, and were not ashamed."

When Adam says a man shall leave his father and mother, we wonder how Adam knows this is what happens afterwards. Did he know that this was a picture of God's Church?

Ephesians 5:31-32 "For this cause shall a man leave his father and mother, and shall be joined unto his wife, and they two shall be one flesh. This is a great mystery: but I speak concerning Christ and the church."

Christ and the Church become one flesh. We are in Him and He is in us. Consider this:

Gen 2:24 "Therefore shall a man leave his father and mother..."

Why does he leave? To be "one flesh."

Eph 5: 31 "For this cause shall a man leave his father and mother..."

Why does he leave? To be "one flesh."

To be "one flesh" with Christ is to be part of His church. This woman is to be one flesh with Adam (a man of God) and be under his spiritual leadership. This way, there will be no shame over their *nakedness.*

Romans 5:14 "Nevertheless death reigned from Adam to Moses, even over them that had not sinned after the similitude of Adam's transgression, who is the figure of him that was to come."

Adam in the Garden of Eden is a *figure* of the man of God. A *figure* of a Prophet who brings the Word of God to others. A *figure* of a Pastor who oversees his Church. In order to do this, God must first qualify them or (make them in His Image.)

Genesis 1:27 "So God created man in his own image, in the image of God created he him; male and female created he them."

Man created in His image is the Spiritual authority. [I believe that these are the 1/3 elect chosen before the foundation of the world. They are to bring the True Gospel to the rest of the world (2/3's or 666). The male and female (created he them) are those in the world that will either become sheep or become goats]

God had to create a man of God first. Prepare him (in His Image), and give him dominion over many things. The congregation is placed under his spiritual leadership. It is a good working system. But then something happens in the Garden of Eden to alter this.

Matthew 13:25 "But while men slept, his enemy came and sowed tares among the wheat, and went his way."

Adam *slept.* And the next thing he knew, he had a wife. This wife of his will change things around in the Garden of Eden.

The Curse In The Garden

Genesis 3:1 "Now the serpent was more subtil than any beast of the field which the LORD God had made."

In order to fully comprehend the spiritual curses given to those in the Garden of Eden, we must first understand what the "beast of the field" is. To help us do this we need to look up several key words that are used in this verse. First we define the more common words, and then we compare Scripture with Scripture. What is the field?

(O.T.) Field #7704 from an unused root-to spread out; a field (as flat)

(N.T.) Field #68 a field (as a drive for cattle); generally the country; specifically a farm

Jesus Christ tells us what the field is in the Book of Matthew.

Matthew 13:38 "The field is the world; the good seed are the children of the kingdom; but the tares are the children of the wicked one;"

God created an area (a field) to work out His Salvation Plan. This is where the *beast* is.

Beast #2416 Alive; hence, raw (flesh); fresh (plant, water, year), strong; also (as noun especially in the feminine singular & masculine plural) life (or living thing)

Many people believe that the "any beast of the field" is talking about the literal animal kingdom. Satan is or he possesses a serpent of this field in order to talk to the woman.

Is this what is going on? Is the beast in this verse referring to the animal kingdom?

OLD TESTAMENT BEAST (S)

#929 properly a dumb beast; any large quadruped or animal (often collect.) [to be mute]

#1165 cattle [from 1197 (in the sense of eating) to kindle, i.e. consume]

#2123 (unused root) to be conspicuous; fullness of the breast; also a moving creature

#2423 an animal [from 2418 to live]

#2966 prey, i.e. flocks devoured by animals [feminine collect. of 2964 something torn]

#3753 a dromedary (from its rapid motion as if dancing) [from 3769 to dance (whirl)]

#4806 stall-fed; often (as noun) beeves [from 4754 "whip" grossness, of domineering]

#5038 a flabby thing, i.e. a carcass or carrion (human or bestial) fig. an idol

#5315 properly a breathing creature, i.e. animal of vitality [from 5314 to breathe]

#6728 a desert-dweller, i.e. nomad or wild beast [same as 6723 to parch; aridity, a desert]

#7409 a relay of animals on a post-route (as stored up for that purpose); by impl. Courser

There are several definitions from the above (beast) list that would have been a more accurate choice to describe these (animal kingdom) or the (possessed snake) beliefs.

Because we know that the serpent is Satan. And Satan is a spirit being. Is it possible that God is using *beast* to describe Satan as a spiritual animal? Who seeks to mislead us? As with Dragon, Lion, or Beelzebub, God utilizes different names to describe Satan's roles.

Beast #2416 Alive; hence, raw (flesh); fresh (plant, water, year), strong; also (as noun especially in the feminine singular & masculine plural) life (or living thing)

#2416 describes raw life or freshly given life. It is described as strong. Note that as a noun, it is in the feminine singular & masculine plural. That is significant information, as we will find out later. Beast best describes something that is connected to the spirit world.

Ezekiel 10:20 "This is the living creature that I saw under the God of Israel by the river of Chebar; and I knew that they were the cherubims."

Living Creature #2416 Alive; hence, raw (flesh); fresh (plant, water, year), strong; also (as noun especially in the feminine singular & masculine plural) life (or living thing)

Genesis 3:24 "So he drove out the man; and he placed at the east of the garden of Eden Cherubims, and a flaming sword which turned every way, to keep the way of the tree of life."

Life #2416 Alive; hence, raw (flesh); fresh (plant, water, year), strong; also (as noun especially in the feminine singular & masculine plural) life (or living thing)

We see a description of a spiritual being (beast), a description of the cherubims (living creature), and a spiritual description of living for all Eternity (tree of Life). They all are expressed as having life or being alive. The spiritual world has *life*. And God uses earthly descriptions in Scripture to describe spiritual beings and spiritual concepts to us.

When is a beast (#2416) not a beast (#929) even though it says it is a beast?

Leviticus 11:1-2 "And the LORD spake unto Moses and to Aaron, saying unto them, Speak unto the children of Israel, saying, These are the beasts (#2416) which ye shall eat among all the beasts (#929) that are on the earth."

God is teaching Israel that literal beasts of the earth can represent spiritual cleanliness.

Ezekiel 14:21 "For thus saith the Lord GOD; How much more when I send my four sore judgments upon Jerusalem, the sword, and the famine, and the noisome beast (#2416), and the pestilence, to cut off from it man and beast (#929)?"

Noisome #7451 bad or (as noun) evil (naturally or morally) [from 7489 to spoil (break into pieces); to make (or be) good for nothing; bad (physically, socially, morally)]

God tells *certain* elders of Israel (the spiritual leaders of that day) that He will send (4) judgments upon Jerusalem. These are spiritual judgments that are manifested in physical ways. All of these judgments focus on a spiritual separation from God. While the sword, famine, and pestilence can be more easily understood (in a spiritual sense) as God taking away the Word from them, the noisome beast here does the same. As the serpent who is identified with the beast in Genesis 3:1 will deceive the woman, the noisome beasts in Ezekiel 14 will do likewise upon Jerusalem. Who are these beasts?

In the Book of Revelation chapter 17, God describes to us who this beast is.

Beast #2342 a dangerous animal; diminutive from the same as [2339 hunting, i.e. (figuratively) destruction]

Revelation 17:3 "So he carried me away in the spirit into the wilderness: and I saw a woman sit upon a scarlet coloured beast, full of names of blasphemy, having seven heads and ten horns."

In Revelation chapter 12, a woman flees or flies into the wilderness for a period of time. In Revelation 17 we see that she went through some changes during that duration. Through all of the blood of the saints and martyrs she became drunken. She became a great whore. But it is the beast that she sits on that is our focus here. Verse 7 tells us the beast has seven heads and ten horns. Verse 9 tells us the seven heads are 7 mountains and verse 12 that the ten horns are 10 kings. They shall make war with the

Lamb (verse 14). This beast is identified with mankind's timeline on earth.

Revelation 17:1b "...Come hither; I will shew unto thee the judgment of the great whore that sitteth upon many waters:"

I thought that the great whore sat on a beast? She does sit on a beast. But this *beast* rises out of the sea. We read about this in Revelation chapter 13.

Revelation 13:1 "And I stood upon the sand of the sea, and saw a beast rise up out of the sea, having seven heads and ten horns, and upon his horns ten crowns, and upon his heads the name of blasphemy."

God is associating the beast with the many waters. What does "many waters" mean?

Revelation 17:15-17 "And he saith unto me, The waters which thou sawest, where the whore sitteth, are peoples, and multitudes, and nations, and tongues. And the ten horns which thou sawest upon the beast, these shall hate the whore, and shall make her desolate and naked, and shall eat her flesh, and burn her with fire. For God hath put in their hearts to fulfil his will, and to agree, and give their kingdom unto the beast, until the words of God shall be fulfilled."

The spiritual *marriage* of mankind and the serpent is identified as the beast. Beast is used here to identify Satan's role with man during this time. As the Spirit of God resides in a man of God (who is the bride of Christ), the spirit of antichrist also resides in the hearts and minds of the beast. The man of God is in the Image of God; the man of the world is in the image of the beast. This is the *beast* that is described in Revelation 17. The serpent/mankind marriage is the beast that comes out of the Sea, out of the Earth, and the image of that beast. Note that this image of the beast, is created by the beast of the earth to make mankind worship the beast of the sea (who is given a deadly wound.)

Genesis 3:1 "Now the serpent was more subtil than any beast of the field which the LORD God had made."

Beast #2416 Alive; hence, raw (flesh); fresh (plant, water, year), strong; also (as noun especially in the feminine singular & masculine plural) life (or living thing)

Again #2416 describes strong raw life or freshly given life. It best describes God's spiritual kingdom. When this raw life combines with a woman or men, it is called a beast. (The spirit of this beast always leads.) Now in this spirit world, the serpent (or Satan) was the most subtil of all of God's raw life creations. Who is this Satan?

(O.T.) #7854 an opponent; especially (with the article prefix) Satan, the archenemy of good [from 7853 a primitive root; to attack, (fig) accuse]

(N.T.) #4567 the accuser, i.e. the devil [corresponding to 4566 Satan, i.e. the Devil]

The term Satan is identified with a purpose, an opponent, and a force against good.

But Satan is identified as a serpent in Genesis 3:1. Why? What is this serpent?

Serpent #5175 a snake (from its hiss) [from 5172 primitive root; properly to hiss, i.e. whisper a (magic) spell; generally to prognosticate]

The serpent is identified by the sound it makes. The sound that it makes is identified with "whisper a (magic) spell." People believe that Satan *possessed* a serpent to be able to talk to the woman, but Satan talks to us today, he tempts us as he did Jesus. He doesn't need to possess an animal to do this. He is a spirit being that communicates to us just as he communicated to the woman in the garden. The big difference is that Adam and the woman were not spiritually changed as yet. Their perceiving the presence of God and communicating to Him (and the serpent) were different. But this would soon be changed. The focus here is how the serpent talked to her. When I am tempted to do a sin, I do not talk to an animal and debate it. I debate it in my heart and in my mind. So did the woman. That is where the serpent will battle the woman. He will be *subtil* (try to make her bare).

Subtil #6175 cunning (usually in a bad sense) passive participle of [6191 to be (or make) bare; but used only in the derivative sense to be cunning (usually in a bad sense)]

The Serpent is more subtil than devil(s) (N.T.) #1139, #1140; (O.T.) #7700. We don't stand a chance against this spiritual force. This force always wins. We need the Spirit of God (to guard our hearts and minds) for each and every battle or we will never succeed.

Consider Paul's warning to the Church at Corinth.

2 Corinthians 11:3 "But I fear, lest by any means, as the serpent beguiled Eve through his subtilty, so your minds should be corrupted from the simplicity that is in Christ."

He warns that the serpent will try to corrupt their minds as he did with Eve. Christ's Gospel message is pure and direct. The serpent will always try to confuse its simplicity. In Genesis we can see how the serpent beguiled the woman to see things his way.

Beguiled #1818 to seduce wholly [from 1537 origin from & 538 to cheat, i.e. delude]

Genesis 3:2-3 "And he said unto the woman, Yea, hath God said, Ye shall not eat of every tree of the garden? And the woman said unto the serpent, We may eat of the fruit of the trees of the garden: But of the fruit of the tree which is in the midst of the garden, God hath said, Ye shall not eat of it, neither shall ye touch it, lest ye die."

The serpent goes to the woman because he knows that the man Adam is made in the Image of God. There is little chance of deceiving the man into obeying him. The woman however, is a *step away* from the direct creation. God created her from a creation. This creation is the weaker vessel. Satan's goal was to have the woman disobey God's direct command to not eat of the Tree of good and evil. Why? And why did God allow this to happen? We do know that God has a Salvation plan for mankind. And that He has chosen His Elect before the World was created. And the description of the female species indicates that she is ready (to know) the male species. There is a *matrix* for mankind. And so children were part of the plan.

None of this caught God by surprise. He allowed this to happen. It is for His purpose.

The serpent goes to her and begins his deception. He directs her focus on something she should not be focusing on. The Tree that is in the midst of the garden. In verse 6, she eats of it. Her focus never left the tree that the serpent directed her to. Please note that this happens before God curses her. Her spiritual condition was susceptible to this kind of attack from the serpent. She was the weaker vessel from the start via her creation. Her answer to the serpent includes the additional command of "neither shall ye touch it". She adds to the Law of God. Isn't this what the Pharisees did in the Temple? Added a bunch of extra rules? Those spiritual leaders understanding of who is really in charge was very apparent. They were. And it is the same for the woman here. She is ready to believe anything that the serpent tells her. Even if the serpent calls God a liar.

Genesis 3:4-5 "And the serpent said unto the woman, Ye shall not surely die: For God doth know that in the day ye eat thereof, then your eyes shall be opened, and ye shall be as gods, knowing good and evil."

The Serpent says God is a liar. Then he promises the woman wisdom equal to the gods. She doesn't question what she is told. She accepts the word of the serpent as truth.

Genesis 3:6 "And when the woman saw that the tree was good for food, and that it was pleasant to the eyes, and a tree to be desired to make one wise, she took of the fruit thereof, and did eat, and gave also unto her husband with her; and he did eat."

The woman agrees with the serpent. She concludes in her *mind* that this is not a sin. (Despite God's command, the tree is now allowed for food.) She feels in her *heart* that this is right. The woman also believed that there was something missing in her life.

Philippians 4:6-7 "Be careful for nothing; but in every thing by prayer and supplication with thanksgiving let your requests be made known unto God. And the peace of God, which passeth all understanding, shall keep your hearts and minds through Christ Jesus."

This passage in Philippians is an instruction of how to resist the Devil. If you follow this, you will "keep your hearts and minds through Christ Jesus" and not lose them to the evil in this world. Genesis 3:6 illustrates of the birth of a sin in a person. God has created us to confront evil in this world through our hearts and minds. That is the battleground. The woman loses this battle. And because she lost this battle, she puts Adam in a position where he has to decide between his wife and God. Adam was supposed to guard/tend the garden. He should have stopped the woman (if he could) or he should have refused the fruit she offered. Instead he receives the 'first supper' given by the woman (as opposed to the last supper) in the garden. Adam has now become the help meet (or the woman). The woman has now become the man of God. This was the serpent's purpose all along. To get to the man of God, get to them first who are under his spiritual authority.

Genesis 3:7 "And the eyes of them both were opened, and they knew that they were naked; and they sewed fig leaves together, and made themselves aprons."

Eyes #5869 a primitive word; an eye (lit or fig); by analogy a fountain (eye of landscape)

Opened #6491 a primitive root; to open (the senses, especially the eyes); to be observant.

God created Adam and the woman. They did not experience a *birth* per se, but were given life. This life included a sinless spiritual state of being. For Adam and the woman, this state of being had a direct access to God. When their eyes were opened, a separation from Him has taken place. To me this is a description of their *earthly birth*. A person's eyes are closed to begin with (there is no awareness of this world's sinful nature), and then the person is born. Their eyes are now opened to this world and they sense their sinful reality.

When the person dies, their eyes close again and they are in the presence of God. (One way or another.) This verse describes Adam and the woman's birth into this reality. The reality we all face at birth. The first thing they both realize is that they are *naked*.

Naked #5903 nudity [from 6191 to be (or make) bare; but used only in the derivative sense to be cunning (usually in a bad sense)]

Subtil #6175 cunning (usually in a bad sense) passive participle of [6191 to be (or make) bare; but used only in the derivative sense to be cunning (usually in a bad sense)]

The Strong's concordance lists 7 definitions for the word naked in the Old Testament. You can be naked in many different ways. Note that Adam and the woman's nakedness resemble the *subtil* way of the serpent. Satan wanted to make Adam and the woman naked, but not because he wanted to see their bodies. He wanted the spiritual *covering* of God to be striped away from them. They are now spiritually naked in the sight of God. A real separation between the Creator and His creation has taken place. I believe that they knew that this is what happened to them. Man's perception of God now includes fear and shame. They will now try to hide from Him both spiritually and physically. By using the leaves from a fig tree.

Fig #8384 (in the singular feminine) the fig (tree or fruit)

Leaves #5929 a leaf (as coming up on a tree); collectively foliage [from 5927 to ascend]

Aprons #2290 a belt (for the waist) [from 2296 primitive root; to gird on (as belt, armor)]

These fig leaves that Adam and the woman *sewed* together to literally cover them, spiritually represent a replacement for the covering that God had provided. A covering they rejected through disobedience. This covering is feminine based (because of the fig tree used.) Any *feminine covering* is not acceptable to God. This is because:

1 Corinthians 11:3 "But I would have you know, that the head of every man is Christ; and the head of the woman is the man; and the head of Christ is God."

The husband (Adam) is the head of the wife (woman). Both Adam and the woman had changed this relationship. This brings God to the garden. He knows they have disobeyed.

Genesis 3:8 "And they heard the voice of the LORD God walking in the garden in the cool of the day: and Adam and his wife hid themselves from the presence of the LORD God amongst the trees of the garden."

Adam and his wife now use some of this new nakedness knowledge (cunning). They hide themselves amongst the trees of the garden, by covering themselves with leaves. They try to pass themselves off as a *tree* of the garden, because they don't want the presence (face) of the LORD God upon them. So He will talk to them. He calls out to Adam by name.

Called #7121 to call out to (i.e. properly address by name, but used in a wide variety)

Genesis 3:9-13 "And the LORD God called unto Adam, and said unto him, Where art thou? And he said, I heard thy voice in the garden, and I was afraid, because I was naked; and I hid myself. And he said, Who told thee that thou wast naked? Hast thou eaten of the tree, whereof I commanded thee that thou shouldest not eat? And the man said, The woman whom thou gavest to be with me, she gave me of the tree, and I did eat. And the LORD God said unto the woman, What is this that thou hast done? And the woman said, The serpent beguiled me, and I did eat."

He didn't really need to ask where they where, this was to illustrate a spiritual point.

God asks Adam what has happened. He tells Him the truth. God asks the woman what has happened. She tells Him the truth. Notice that God doesn't ask the serpent anything.

Adam and the woman have now *confessed* their sin before the LORD God. He will now set boundaries and re-direct the desires of the serpent, the man, and the woman. These limits will continue in His creation throughout all time. He begins with the serpent.

Genesis 3:14 "And the LORD God said unto the serpent, Because thou hast done this, thou art cursed above all cattle, and above every beast of the field; upon thy belly shalt thou go, and dust shalt thou eat all the days of thy life"

Cursed #779 primitive root: to execrate

Belly #1512 the external abdomen, belly (as the source of the fetus) [probably from 1518 to gush forth (as water), generally to issue]

Dust #6083 dust (as powdered or gray); hence, clay, earth, mud [from 6080 to be gray or perhaps rather to pulverize; to be dust]

What you started with mankind, you are *cursed* to finish. Satan is cursed above all cattle (representing the literal flesh) and every beast (representing the spiritual flesh). God intertwines the serpent with mankind until he is destroyed in the Lake of Fire. God sets a limit in how he can influence mankind, (upon thy belly shalt thou go) and also directs his desire (dust shalt thou eat all the days of thy life) to do the job given him.

Proverbs 13:25 "The righteous eateth to the satisfying of his soul: but the belly of the wicked shall want."

Many believe that as God curses the serpent, He is restricting him to this earth. No more traveling to Heaven. Is this true? Is he stuck here on earth? What about in the Book of Job? Satan is able to go "to and fro." He is able to come into the presence of the LORD with the sons of God. Most believe that the LORD is in Heaven there. Therefore, it is at the cross where Satan is limited strictly to earth. "Upon thy Belly" is the *method* given to the serpent that he can use to devour mankind (dust). What does this mean? In the next verse we read about the *seed* of Satan. As the seed of the woman is produced from the belly of the woman, so then the seed of the serpent comes from the belly of the beast. Isn't it interesting that we are born wicked, speaking lies like our father, the Devil?

Genesis 3:15a "And I will put enmity between thee and the woman,"

Enmity #342 Hostility [from #340 a primitive root; to hate (as one of an opposite tribe or party); hence, to be hostile]

It is important not to miss this. God places *two* curses between the serpent and the woman. First, He puts enmity between this serpent and womankind. He directs Satan's desire to destroy God's creation more on the woman than on the man. It is fitting, being that the serpent already tried this method and had succeeded.

Genesis 3:15b "and between thy seed and her seed;"

Seed #2233 Seed; (fig) fruit, plant, sowing time, posterity [from #2232 a primitive root; to sow; (fig) to disseminate, plant, fructify]

God also puts enmity (spiritual hatred) between Satan's seed and the woman's seed. Is this enmity between the seeds all of the woman's seed or just a special remnant of it?

Revelation 12:17 "And the dragon was wroth with the woman, and went to make war with the remnant of her seed, which keep the commandments of God, and have the testimony of Jesus Christ."

The *seed* of the woman that keeps the commandments of God (the remnant), it is them that the beast will war against with his seed. Remember how beast was defined earlier?

Beast #2416 Alive; hence, raw (flesh); fresh (plant, water, year), strong; also (as noun especially in the feminine singular & masculine plural) life (or living thing)

#2416 describes raw life or freshly given life. Described as strong. Note that as a noun, it is in the feminine singular & masculine plural. Beast classified in the *feminine singular* and in the *masculine plural.* This beast will attack us as described above. He attacked Adam in this manner through the woman (in the feminine singular).

But who are the seed of Satan? Scripture tells us who the children (seed) of the Devil are.

John 8:44 "Ye are of your father the devil, and the lusts of your father ye will do. He was a murderer from the beginning, and abode not in the truth, because there is no truth in him. When he speaketh a lie, he speaketh of his own: for he is a liar, and the father of it."

1 John 3:9-10 "Whosoever is born of God doth not commit sin; for his seed remaineth in him: and he cannot sin, because he is born of God. In this the children of God are manifest, and the children of the devil: whosoever doeth not righteousness is not of God, neither he that loveth not his brother."

The Bible describes two armies (two seeds). The seed of the Devil are these *Pharisees* and *False Prophets.* The Dragon through them makes war with the seed that keep the testimony of Jesus Christ.

Genesis 3:15c " it shall bruise thy head, and thou shalt bruise his heel."

Bruise #7779 a primitive root; properly to gape, i.e. snap at; figuratively to overwhelm

Head #7218 from an unused root apparently meaning to shake; the head (as most easily shaken) whether lit. or fig. (in many applications, of place, time, rank, etc.)

Heel #6119 Heel (as protuberant); hence, a track, the rear (of a army) [from #6117 to swell out or up, to seize by the heel; figuratively to circumvent (as if tripping up the heels); also, to restrain (as if holding by the heel]

The bruising that goes on between the head and heel are also assumed to be a spiritual picture of the battle between Christ and Satan. That is a correct conclusion. But because the word seed (the same word that God used when speaking to Abraham when promising his covenant to them in Genesis 17:7) means the actual offspring of peoples, nations, and tribes, this bruising will be done between the two factions. Those who are the seed of Christ will battle those who are the seed of the Devil. Note: neither one will actually have a physical offspring- this is a spiritual family. And Jesus tells us who His family is.

Matthew 12:48-50 "But he answered and said unto him that told him, Who is my mother? and who are my brethren? And he stretched forth his hand toward his disciples, and said, Behold my mother and my brethren! For whosoever shall do the will of my Father which is in heaven, the same is my brother, and sister, and mother."

Head and heel are not literal places that will be bruised on actual *children* but represent assaults on the strongholds of each tribe. The head of the serpent will be (overwhelmed or bruised) in many places in the world, all throughout the time of mankind, against any position taken by man (rank). The heel of the seed of Christ will be bruised near the end of time as God's seed disappears, allowing Satan to restrain and overwhelm in the end.

Revelation 13:7 "And it was given unto him to make war with the saints, and to overcome them: and power was given him over all kindreds, and tongues, and nations."

Do we read anywhere in the Bible where Satan's head (as the beast) is bruised? In the Book of Romans, Paul writes a letter to his fellow *seeds* in Rome.

Romans 16:20 "And the God of peace shall bruise Satan under your feet shortly. The Grace of our Lord Jesus Christ be with you. Amen."

All bruising requires a spirit behind it. For the seed of Christ, they need the God of Peace to do this bruising. For the seed of the serpent, they need the spirit of Satan.

Genesis 3:16 "Unto the woman he said, I will greatly multiply thy sorrow (#6093) and thy conception; in sorrow (#6089) thou shalt bring forth children; and thy desire shall be to thy husband, and he shall rule over thee."

Sorrow #6093 worrisomeness, i.e. labor or pain [from 6087 to carve, i.e. fabricate or fashion; hence, (in a bad sense) to worry, pain or anger]

Sorrow #6089 an earthen vessel; usually (painful) toil; also a pang (whether of body or mind [from 6087 carve, fabricate, fashion; hence, (in a bad sense) to worry, pain, anger]

Conception #2032 pregnancy [from 2029 to be (or become) pregnant, conceive (lit/fig)]

Desire #8669 a longing [from 7783 (to run after or over, i.e. overflow) in the original Sense of stretching out after]

Rule #4910 a primitive root; to rule

God will now curse the woman. The woman has a pre-condition remember, God has placed an enmity between her and the serpent. That affects her as well as all women. He multiplies in her two things. Sorrow and conception. The (6093) Sorrow is an increase in *worrisomeness*. Adam will also be cursed by God with this sorrow in Genesis 3:17.

The (6089) sorrow strictly deals with the conception (the actual giving birth to children).

"In sorrow thou shalt bring forth children" God places women in a Planned Godhood program. The woman was created out of the man, and now out of the woman, the creation will come from. (In a painful earthen vessel you will bring forth children.)

In the garden, there were no problems, no worries for Adam and the woman. Then sin entered. Adam and the woman became afraid. They worried about the presence of God and they tried to hide from him. (They tried to *separate* themselves from Him.) This separation from God brings worrisomeness or sorrow. Sin brought on the initial worrisomeness or sorrow. God will now greatly *multiply* this sorrow for the woman. In essence, God is withdrawing His presence further from her. This will increase her spiritual sorrow. She is going to need some help with her relationship to God. So He directs her *desire* to her husband, and he is to rule over the wife. Remember, she desired to be wiser. This was not where God wanted her desires to go. As the LORD directed the desire of the serpent (dust thou shalt eat), He also directs the desire of the woman (to thy husband). This is because of the *angels*.

Ephesians 5:22-23 "Wives, submit yourselves unto your own husbands, as unto the Lord. For the husband is the head of the wife, even as Christ is the head of the church: and he is the saviour of the body."

In Ephesians, Paul reiterates what God tells the woman here. This is why the husband is the head of the wife. This is why God can compare the man to the "saviour of the body."

This is why the woman must be silent in the church. This is why the woman is called the weaker vessel. This was never man's idea. God set up this system for His own purpose.

Genesis 3:17a "And unto Adam he said, Because thou hast hearkened unto the voice of thy wife, and hast eaten of the tree, of which I commanded thee, saying, Thou shalt not eat of it:"

Hearkened #8085 to hear intelligently (often with implication of attention, obedience)

There are two things that God brings to Adam's attention. He has *hearkened* unto the voice of his wife. And he ate of the tree that he was commanded not to eat. You never really hear a sermon that highlights the fact that Adam *hearkened* to his wife. They just focus on the fact he ate of the fruit. And, that he was somewhat responsible by not stopping this from happening. Men of God today do not understand how to teach this because they do not consider how God created the man and woman. They do not understand the *spiritual limitations* placed upon the man and the woman as He cursed them. Adam listened to his wife's suggestion (command?) and willfully disobeyed God. The woman *usurped authority* over Adam. And he let her do this. He loved his woman more than he loved his God. This is the beginning of a pattern we can see all throughout the Bible. In the Old Testament, we can see this happening in Noah's day and in the lives of King Solomon, Samson, and others. Does this apply for us in the New Testament?

1 Timothy 2:11-14 "Let the woman learn in silence with all subjection. But I suffer not a woman to teach, nor to usurp authority over the man, but to be in silence. For Adam was first formed, then Eve. And Adam was not deceived, but the woman being deceived was in the transgression."

I guess it does. Remember, the book of 1 Timothy was written after Pentecost. After God's Spirit had been poured out upon all flesh. This *pouring out* doesn't negate how He created the man and woman, nor the curse that was given to them. God's creation of man and woman and the spiritual limitations He placed upon them (along with the serpent) are to continue until the rapture, when these fleshly bodies are no longer needed.

Genesis 3:17b "cursed is the ground for thy sake;"

Cursed #779 primitive root: to execrate

Ground #127 soil (from its general redness) [from 119 to show blood (in the face)]

God out of His great love for Adam curses the ground for his sake. We understand on a physical level that God is making Adam work for his food. Instead of just reaching out and taking of the fruit, he must work in his own garden. He will have to sow, tend, and harvest his garden. But Adam is still a spiritual being as well as a fleshly one. This curse from God on how to provide food for his flesh is also instructions on how to feed his spirit.

Did you know that there are 2 basic Old Testament definitions of *ground* among the 8 given in the Strong's Concordance? One of them is very similar to the definition of man.

Ground #127 soil (from its general redness) [from 119 to show blood (in the face), i.e. flush or turn rosy]

Ground #776 from an unused root probably meaning to be firm, the earth (at large, or partitively a land)

Man #120 ruddy, i.e. human being (an individual or the species, mankind, etc…) [from 119 to show blood (in the face) i.e. flush or turn rosy]

When ground mixes with God, it goes through a change. It is set apart from (776) ground, and becomes (127) ground. This is the ground (127) that God makes man out of.

Genesis 2:7 "And the LORD God formed man of the dust of the ground, and breathed into his nostrils the breath of life; and man became a living soul."

We see that the very presence of God changes the ground itself. It becomes Holy ground.

Exodus 3:5 "And he said, Draw not nigh hither: put off thy shoes from off thy feet, for the place whereon thou standest is holy ground (#127)."

We read in the next chapter of Exodus an example of (776) ground. Common ground.

Exodus 4:3 "And he said, Cast it on the ground (#776). And he cast it on the ground (#776), and it became a serpent; and Moses fled from before it."

And in Genesis 3:19, God tells us that we are from dust and that we will return to dust.

Dust #6083 dust (as powered or gray); hence, clay, earth, mud [from 6080 to be gray, dust]

We are formed of the (gray powered) dust of the special ground (soil from its redness) and when given life, are identified with our color (dust with blood = ruddy).

In the New Testament, Jesus also identifies *ground* with an individual created by God.

Matthew 13:23 "But he that received seed into the good ground is he that heareth the word, and understandeth it; which also beareth fruit, and bringeth forth, some an hundredfold, some sixty, some thirty."

I think it is safe to say that we are connected to this (127) type ground, and because of that, God can refer to us here as good ground. But we are also a spiritual being. We are placed in this soil suit (or dress). We are put in this *ground* outfit to wear while we live on this planet Earth. We wear this ground while we *transit* this reality.

Genesis 3:17b "cursed is the ground for thy sake;"

Sake #5668 properly Crossed, i.e. (abstractly) Transit; used only on account of, in order that [passive (voice) participle of 5674 to cross over; used very widely of any transition; specifically to cover (in copulation)]

Cursed is your physical *substance* (for Adam and all of mankind) while you visit earth. This physical substance is set apart from God. As with the woman, this will cause man's spiritual sorrow. This is experienced as long as a person lives on this planet.

Genesis 3:17c "in sorrow shalt thou eat of it all the days of thy life;"

Sorrow #6093 worrisomeness, i.e. labor or pain [from 6087 to carve, i.e. fabricate or fashion; hence, (in a bad sense) to worry, pain or anger]

Man will live on this earth separated from God. As with the flesh (that always hungers for literal food), our spirit will also hunger (experience spiritual sorrow) for God.

Luke 4:4 "And Jesus answered him, saying, It is written, That man shall not live by bread alone, but by every word of God."

Man will now spiritually consume food from the Word in this separated state. There's a good reason we are to suffer this *sorrow*. It is because of the love God has for us.

Proverbs 15:13 "A merry heart maketh a cheerful countenance: but by sorrow of the heart the spirit is broken."

God will break our *spirit* by putting this tribulation upon us. And all of mankind will go through this sorrow. As with the literal ground that we plant seed in is no longer pure (it has thorns and thistles), these thorns and thistles will manifest in our soil (or self) as well.

Genesis 3:18a "Thorns also and thistles shall it bring forth to thee;"

Thorns #6975 a thorn [from 6972 (in the sense of pricking) to clip off; used only as denominative from 7019; to spend the harvest season]

Thistles #1863 a thorn

We easily understand these thorns and thistles as weeds that we must deal with while we grow our crops. We must put physical effort into our garden in order for it to produce fruit. It is the same for our spiritual fruit. Thorns and thistles are placed in our way. They are *spiritual weeds* we must deal with as we seek God. As we seek His Truth. God uses these thorns and thistles to test us, to direct us, to chastise us. Paul identifies one of these thorns as a messenger of Satan. From within and without, we face thorns and thistles.

2 Corinthians 12:7 "And lest I should be exalted above measure through the abundance of the revelations, there was given to me a thorn in the flesh, the messenger of Satan to buffet me, lest I should be exalted above measure."

God uses thorns and thistles in Scripture to show that they are a spiritual force that is in opposition to mankind re-connecting to God. We must face our own thorns and thistles.

Isaiah 32:13 "Upon the land of my people shall come up thorns and briers; yea, upon all the houses of joy in the joyous city:"

Jeremiah 4:3 "For thus saith the LORD to the men of Judah and Jerusalem, Break up your fallow ground, and sow not among thorns."

Ezekiel 28:24 "And there shall be no more a pricking brier unto the house of Israel, nor any grieving thorn of all that are round about them, that despised them; and they shall know that I am the Lord GOD."

In Mark, we are given a description of how thorns and thistles personally relate to us.

Mark 4:18-19 "And these are they which are sown among thorns; such as hear the word, And the cares of this world, and the deceitfulness of riches, and the lusts of other things entering in, choke the word, and it becometh unfruitful."

This *ground* was in need of a good gardener. Their thorns took over any understanding of the Word of God. The Word was *choked*. No harvest, no fruit. No love for their Creator.

Genesis 3:18b "and thou shalt eat the herb of the field;"

Herb #6212 to glisten (or be green); grass (or any tender shoot)

Spiritually this represents the minute knowledge of the LORD each human being receives, proving to them the existence of God. This is why we are all without *excuse*.

This living soul of ours needs this *spiritual herb* to exist, just as our flesh needs the physical herb to live. In Genesis 1:30, God tells us that everything that lives is given this green herb for meat. Spiritually this green herb that sustains our soul is of God. It is a continuous life giving connection between Him and His creation.

Genesis 1:30 "And to every beast of the earth, and to every fowl of the air, and to every thing that creepeth upon the earth, wherein there is life, I have given every green herb for meat: and it was so."

Once Adam and the woman could eat of the fruit of the trees in the garden. Now Adam and the woman are put on the green herb diet. Adam eats what everybody else eats.

This will never satisfy the man of God. They are made in the Image of Him. This herb will never be enough. They want to know God more. But this will now require effort.

Genesis 3:19 "In the sweat of thy face shalt thou eat bread, till thou return unto the ground; for out of it wast thou taken: for dust thou art, and unto dust shalt thou return."

Sweat #2188 perspiration [from 2111 to shake off, (fig) to agitate (as with fear)-in the sense of 3154 to ooze]

Face #639 properly the nose or nostril; hence, the face, and occasionally a person; also (from the rapid breathing in passion) ire [from 599 to breath hard, i.e. be enraged]

Bread #3899 food (for man or beast), especially bread or grain (for making it) [from 3898 to feed on; (fig) to consume; by implication to battle (as destruction)]

Dust #6083 dust (as powered or gray); hence, clay, earth, mud [from 6080 to be gray, dust]

Bread is much more sustaining than the *herb* of the field. The focus here is on the effort now needed to (eat) more than this free herb given to us by God. To be one of His Elect, we need more than just herb. We need the *Bread of Life*. And this bread will come at a price. Remember that God has put enmity between the seeds. The Dragon will make war with them. Through the Beast of the sea and the Beast of the earth he will make war with those who keep the testimony of Jesus Christ. And this war is also fought inside of us. We will get a spiritual workout. We will "sweat." Not like Jesus in the Garden of Gethsemane, but nevertheless, we also will sweat connecting with our God. When we look at the word face (639), it appears we are fed this bread through our nose. Do we receive anything else from God in this manner? It is interesting that we are made this way.

Genesis 2:7 "And the LORD God formed man of the dust of the ground, and breathed into his nostrils the breath of life; and man became a living soul."

And so all of the changes that God instilled in the man and the woman and the serpent are completed. Each has received spiritual limitations. The serpent (upon his belly-this is the method of how he may interact with mankind), the woman (her sorrow multiplied-she now is put in a vulnerable spiritual position), and the man (sweat needed to eat bread and to provide for his family). In addition, all three of their desires are changed. The serpent (dust only for food), the woman (to her husband for spiritual protection), and the man (the desire for bread). These limitations on God's creations are to last until Christ returns.

Genesis 3:20-21 "And Adam called his wife's name Eve; because she was the mother of all living. Unto Adam also and to his wife did the LORD God make coats of skins, and clothed them."

Eve #2332 life-giver; Chavvah (or Eve) [from 2331 to live; by impl. to declare or show]

Mother #517 primitive word; mother (as the bond of the family); in a wide sense (lit/fig)

Adam continues to give names out. He calls his wife Eve. He knows that she will have conception and bring forth children, so he gives her a name that is appropriate.

Coats #3801 from an unused root meaning to cover; a shirt [comp 3802 to clothe]

Skins #5785 skin (as naked); by implication hide, leather [from 5783 to (be) bare]

Clothed #3847 wrap around, i.e. (by implication) to put on a garment or clothe oneself, or another. (lit. or fig.)

The LORD God makes coats of skins to cover Adam and Eve. Was this an Old Testament sacrifice (made to Himself), and from these dead animals He created their clothes? And did He show Adam this sacrifice so that he could pass this down to Cain and Abel? I believe that this is an incorrect assumption. Isn't Adam and Eve's sin as with all the sins ever committed by mankind taken care of by Christ's sacrifice on the cross? If this is incorrect, then what exactly are these "coats of skins?" Could it be our actual skin that covers our flesh?

Job 10:9 "Remember, I beseech thee, that thou hast made me as the clay; and wilt thou bring me into dust again?"

Job 10:11 "Thou hast clothed me with skin and flesh, and hast fenced me with bones and sinews."

When reviewing *skin* in the Bible, it seems that if the skin is from an animal, God will let us know which one (bullock, skin of the burnt offering, heifer, rams, badgers) is used.

Ezekiel 37:6 "And I will lay sinews upon you, and will bring up flesh upon you, and cover you with skin, and put breath in you, and ye shall live; and ye shall know that I am the LORD."

I believe that God (in preparing Adam and Eve for this field) clothed them with the skin that we have today. They are ready to live outside the Garden of Eden, to be tested by this world; they are physically prepared for the temptations of the *flesh*.

Genesis 3:22 "And the LORD God said, Behold, the man is become as one of us, to know good and evil: and now, lest he put forth his hand, and take also of the tree of life, and eat, and live for ever:"

"The man is become as one of us." Man does not become God here. It states, "The man is become as one of us, to know good and evil." Man now has some understanding of good and evil as the LORD does. But because God's plan does not include any sinful flesh existing forever, He cannot allow Adam to eat of the Tree of Life. If Adam is to be saved by Christ, then he must die.

Genesis 3:23 "Therefore the LORD God sent him forth from the garden of Eden, to till the ground (#127) from whence he was taken."

Till #5647 primitive root; to work (in any sense); by implication to serve, till, (causative) enslave, etc.

Ground #127 soil (from its general redness) [from 119 to show blood (in the face)]

He was taken from (127) soil. Therefore, he must "till the ground." The man will now be responsible for the spiritual choices he makes from now on. He must till his soil (or self), and deal with the thorns and thistles that will test him. If the man of God is given a *flock* to shepherd, then he must till that *soil* as well.

Genesis 3:24 "So he drove out the man; and he placed at the east of the garden of Eden Cherubims, and a flaming sword which turned every way, to keep the way of the tree of life."

"To keep the way of the tree of life." What is this *way* of the tree of life?

Keep/guard #8104 a primitive root; properly to hedge about (as with thorns), i.e. guard; generally to protect, attend to, etc.

Way #1870 a road (as trodden); fig. a course of life or mode of action, often adverbially [from 1869 to tread, by implication to walk; also to string a bow (by treading on it)]

Tree #6086 a tree (from its firmness); hence, wood (plural) sticks [from 6095 to fasten (or make firm) i.e. to close (the eyes)]

Life #2416 Alive; hence, raw (flesh); fresh (plant, water, year), strong; also (as noun especially in the feminine singular & masculine plural) life (or living thing)

There was a purity of life in Eden that God will not allow to be changed in any way. This life is from God. It is pure and sinless. This life is God. This state of purity must remain. So God will put a hedge around this garden (as with thorns). Adam is separated from the Garden of Eden where this life is abundant. He is separated from the presence of God. In a sense, God is tending to His garden. He is pulling out the *weeds* that don't belong.

So God drives Adam and Eve away from the garden. A divorce. And God gets the house!

Drove #1644 a primitive root; to drive out from a possession; especially to expatriate or divorce

Eden #5731 Eden, the region of Adam's home [the same as 5730 (masculine) pleasure]

To keep this way of life, God utilizes two heavenly creations. Cherubims and a Flaming Sword.

Flaming #3858 a blaze; also (from the idea of enwrapping) magic (as covert) [from 3857 properly to lick, i.e. (by implication) to blaze

Sword #2719 drought; also a cutting instrument (from its destructive effect) as a knife, sword [from 2717 to parch (through drought), by analogy to desolate, destroy, kill]

The Sword brings on a drought of the *Life* that was offered in the garden freely. It does this (drought) by its flame. The flame is the method (or how) the sword keeps away our knowledge of this purity. Of our God. Knowledge of our Creator is hidden from us in this manner. This results in a limited spiritual relationship with Him.

Cherubims #3742 a cherub or imaginary figure

In the book of Ezekiel we are given more information on this creation of God.

Ezekiel 10:20 "This is the living creature that I saw under the God of Israel by the river of Chebar; and I knew that they were the cherubims."

The Cherubim is a living creature. We usually see them in pairs. The Bible (in the Book of Ezekiel) describes these creatures and their purpose from a spiritual point of view. In Exodus, God commands a physical representation of them to be made for the Ark. Both of these examples show us their purpose. Both the Ark and the Garden of Eden are places where God communicates directly to us humans. Because we are separated from Him, He sets up spiritual barricades. The cherubims represent these spiritual barricades. They keep the way of the Tree of Life. This is what the Gospel message does. It keeps the way of life.

Between God and His creation, is Jesus Christ. He is the Way back to God. And back to Eden where we can live with God. A spiritual divorce needs a spiritual re-marriage.

Genesis 3:6 "And when the woman saw that the tree was good for food, and that it was pleasant to the eyes, and a tree to be desired to make one wise, she took of the fruit thereof, and did eat, and gave also unto her husband with her; and he did eat."

I would like to share a belief of mine here. It is the reason for Adam taking the fruit from the woman and eating it, deliberately disobeying God's command to not eat of it. Why would he do this? Why would he give up all that God gave him in this perfect garden? Didn't he love his God? Or did he love the woman so much he couldn't bear to be without her. He watched her eat this forbidden fruit and knew what would happen to her. She would die. And yet, he still made the decision to eat of the fruit.

Romans 5:14 "Nevertheless death reigned from Adam to Moses, even over them that had not sinned after the similitude of Adam's transgression, who is the figure of him that was to come."

Adam is a figure of him that was to come. The ultimate figure is of course Jesus Christ. So if Adam is a figure of Jesus Christ, then looking at Jesus Christ would give us clues in how to look at Adam and why he took the action he did.

1 John 4:9-10 "In this was manifested the love of God toward us, because that God sent his only begotten Son into the world, that we might live through him. Herein is love, not that we loved God, but that he loved us, and sent his Son to be the propitiation for our sins."

It was love. God loved us. He did not want us to perish. So out of love for us, our Bridegroom joined us (His bride), giving up all of His *reputation* to be with his wife.

Philippians 2:5-9 "Let this mind be in you, which was also in Christ Jesus: Who, being in the form of God, thought it not robbery to be equal with God: But made himself of no reputation, and took upon him the form of a servant, and was made in the likeness of men: And being found in fashion as a man, he humbled himself, and became obedient unto death, even the death of the cross. Wherefore God also hath highly exalted him, and given him a name which is above every name:"

Christ in the form of God (in Spirit and in Life) took on the form of a servant and was made in the likeness of men. He did this out of His love for us (His bride). Adam, out of the love for his *one flesh,* ate of the fruit to be with his wife. He sacrificed his Eden for the woman that God had made for him. He sinned against God doing this. While Jesus never sinned, He still took upon him the sins of those He loves. Adam was made in the image and likeness of God. Because he had great love for this creation, his woman, he was willing to take upon him the sin of the woman. He would spiritually die for her.

The Daughters Of Men

In Genesis chapters one and two, we are taught of the creation of the man and woman.

Genesis 1:27 "So God created man in his own image, in the image of God created he him; male and female created he them."

Image #6754 from an unused root meaning to shade, a phantom, i.e. (fig) illusion, resemblance; hence, a representative

The man created in God's image is Adam. There was no sin in him. A true spiritual representation from its original source (God). He would have had a Christ like mind.

Romans 5:14 "Nevertheless death reigned from Adam to Moses, even over them that had not sinned after the similitude of Adam's transgression, who is the figure of him that was to come."

Figure #5179 a die (as struck), i.e. (by implication) a stamp or scar; by analogy a shape, i.e. a statue (fig) style or resemblance; specifically a sampler ("type"), i.e. model (for imitation) or instance (for warning) [from 5180 a primary verb (in a strengthened form); to "thump", i.e. cudgel or pummel (properly with a stick or bastinado), but in any case by repeated blows; by implication to punish; (fig) to offend (the conscience)]

Adam is a "figure of him that was to come." Many teach that Adam was a representation of Jesus Christ. But he is not God. He is only made in His Image. Therefore, he is spiritually commissioned to represent Him. Adam is a *figure* of a man of God, like a Prophet who brings the Word of God to others, or like an anointed pastor who oversees his church. This is not a physical figure (God is a Spirit, not a human being). So in essence, he is a spiritual shepherd. He was created this way because:

John 4:24 "God is a Spirit: and they that worship him must worship him in spirit and in truth."

God wants Adam (and all those who are of a like figure) to worship Him in spirit as well as in truth. So he must be given knowledge of this truth in order to do so. With this understanding, he can spiritually represent Him. This man Adam was created to do this, to spread God's truth. But he needs someone to preach this truth to. We find that this *someone* comes from within him. God causes a deep sleep to fall upon the man Adam.

Genesis 2:22 "And the rib, which the LORD God had taken from man, made he a woman, and brought her unto the man."

God makes the woman out of Adam's rib. The direct made in the image and after our likeness is done through the body of Adam. This creates a difference in the *image of God* between Adam and the woman. The woman was created out of the man, and now out of the woman, the creation will come from. This is the "male and female created he them."

Genesis 1:27 "So God created man in his own image, in the image of God created he him; male and female created he them."

Male #2145 Remembered, i.e. a male (of man or animals, as being the most noteworthy sex) [from 2142 a primitive root; to mark (so as to be recognized) i.e. to remember; by implication to mention; also to be male]

Female #5347 a female (from the sexual form) [from 5344 a primitive root, to puncture, (literally to perforate, with more or less violence) or fig. to specify, designate, libel]

Look at this as two creations. **"God created man in His own image"** is a line of the men of God that will come from the "male and female" seed. Just like Adam, they will be spiritually created **"in the image of God."** This is the **"created He him."** So out of this first man of God (Adam), God will create mankind. This is the **"male and female created He them."** Out of the male and female will come the children (or seed) of the Serpent. Out of male and female will come the children (or seed) of God. This seed of the serpent will fight the seed of God. This battle of the seeds shows itself immediately with the first children that Adam and Eve produce. We know them as Abel and Cain.

Hebrews 11:4 "By faith Abel offered unto God a more excellent sacrifice than Cain, by which he obtained witness that he was righteous, God testifying of his gifts: and by it he being dead yet speaketh."

Abel is a representation of the man of God. His *faith* witnesses to others. Cain his brother saw this first hand. And we know how he reacted to this witness.

Romans 8:36 "As it is written, For thy sake we are killed all the day long; we are accounted as sheep for the slaughter."

These predestinated men were to be conformed to the image of his son. (Rom 8:29) They were *called* and labeled God's *elect.* (Rom 8:30, 33)

1 Thessalonians 2:15 "Who both killed the Lord Jesus, and their own prophets, and have persecuted us; and they please not God, and are contrary to all men:"

Again, we read those who are made in the image of God will face death and persecution.

Matthew 23:35 "That upon you may come all the righteous blood shed upon the earth, from the blood of righteous Abel unto the blood of Zacharias son of Barachias, whom ye slew between the temple and the altar."

From A to Z the righteous pay a huge price of having this image placed upon them. This is the fate of those created to have this image, to be the seed of God. But what about the seed of the serpent? What about Cain?

1 John 3:12-13 "Not as Cain, who was of that wicked one, and slew his brother. And wherefore slew he him? Because his own works were evil, and his brother's righteous. Marvel not, my brethren, if the world hate you."

Cain is a representation of the seed of the serpent. He is an early example of a Pharisee.

This spiritual battle is a fight to the death. There is *enmity* between the seeds. God placed it there for His purpose, to do His Will. This first battle ended badly for the seed of God. Now we need a replacement. Adam and Eve have another son. Seth.

Seth #8352 put, i.e. substituted; 3rd son of Adam [from 7896 a primitive root: to place]

And so the battle continues. Now we come to the time right before the flood. Mankind has gone through some changes since Adam left Eden. Cain built his own city and named it after his son Enoch. In Genesis chapter 4, we read of a lineage from Cain to Lamech.

In it women and their children are listed. These children are famous (or renown) for what they create. But it is Lamech who kills two men and then declares it a just punishment for the wrongs done to him. This illustrates to us the heart of mankind right before the flood.

Genesis 4:24 "If Cain shall be avenged sevenfold, truly Lamech seventy and sevenfold."

This is what the ungodly believe. Vengeance is mine *saith* Lamech. Jesus disagrees.

Matthew 18:21-22 "Then came Peter to him, and said, Lord, how oft shall my brother sin against me, and I forgive him? till seven times? Jesus saith unto him, I say not unto thee, Until seven times: but, Until seventy times seven."

Notice the difference of attitude in these statements? Why is this? In Genesis chapter 4, we read there about men beginning to call upon the name of the LORD. (Verse 26) The personal knowledge, (or spiritual closeness) that mankind received from God had become more and more distant from them and was slowly being forgotten. Men's hearts turned to themselves for answers. It's a good thing God provided this world with men of God (or sons of God). This was to shepherd us, to help keep us in the Will of God. The Serpent (or Satan) tried to stop the seed of God by rising up his own seed. In Genesis chapter 6, we see this battle of the seeds once again illustrated.

Genesis 6:1 "And it came to pass, when men (#120) began to multiply on the face of the earth (#127), and daughters were born unto them,"

Men #120 ruddy, i.e. human being (an individual or the species, mankind, etc...) [**from 119 to show blood (in the face) i.e. flush or turn rosy**]

Earth #127 soil (from its general redness) [**from 119 to show blood (in the face) i.e. flush or turn rosy**]

As we learned in Genesis 3 where God *cursed* the ground for Adam's sake, that there are two major definitions of ground. When ground mixes with God, it goes through a change. It is set apart from (776) ground, and becomes (127) ground. This is the ground that God makes Adam out of. This (127) ground serves the LORD. Remember, Adam is a *figure* of Him that is to come. So God can identify His seed by using the (127) ground.

Ground #127 soil (from its general redness) [**from 119 to show blood (in the face), i.e. flush or turn rosy**]

Ground #776 from an unused root probably meaning to be firm, the earth (at large, or partitively a land)

Now if we add this understanding to the 2 types of earth that God describes.

Earth #127 soil (from its general redness) [**from 119 to show blood (in the face) i.e. flush or turn rosy**]

Earth #776 from an unused root probable meaning to be firm; the earth (at large, or partitively a land)

When trying to understand spiritual teaching, it is important to see the deeper significance of each word. Most teachers end up teaching 'same word, same meaning' doctrines. Because they do not look up each word (like earth or ground or soil) and then do not compare all those in the Scriptures with the same meaning, they miss the additional depth of what is being taught. They quickly assume that the meaning of the word is the same all throughout the Bible. Thus, their understanding of a doctrine is superficial. The context of the chapter or paragraph is not really understood. God has a serious reason for using (127) earth/ground and not (776) earth/ground. In chapter 6 of Genesis we read (in the earth, on the earth, upon the earth, with the earth, and for the earth.) All of these are the (776) earth that describes every literal physical meaning of the word. God shows us a great example of this use of (127) ground verses the use of (776) ground.

Genesis 8:21 "And the LORD smelled a sweet savour; and the LORD said in his heart, I will not again curse the <u>ground</u> (#127) any more for man's sake; for the imagination of man's heart is evil from his youth; neither will I again smite any more every thing living, as I have done."

God "will not again curse the ground any more" <u>AND</u> "smite any more every thing living as I have done." Does this mean that there are no more thorns and thistles in the ground? Our crops will be like that of the Garden of Eden? No. God will not curse the *ground* any more because the imagination of man's heart is evil from his youth. God proclaims the spiritual state of mankind and shows His Mercy here. AND He won't destroy us like that again (with a flood). This verse in Genesis 8 teaches us that God declares a *spiritual* change (I will not again curse the ground) of his servants. Is this because of what happens to the sons of God in Genesis chapter 6? I believe it does. Remember, we have a ongoing spiritual war between the seeds. And God can and will reference these seeds in Scripture by using variations of the words earth or ground or soil.

Genesis 6:1 "And it came to pass, when men began to multiply on the face of the earth (#127), and daughters were born unto them,"

God uses (127) earth here. He uses (127) again in verse 7. But in verses 4, 5, and 6 God uses (776) earth. He doesn't do this for just physical descriptive instruction. God uses "the face of the earth" both times the (127) earth is used. This is because there is another doctrine involved here. A spiritual application. God uses (127) and (776) in this chapter to give the reader additional information of the world right before the flood. It shows us the *spiritual state* of the earth. The *soil* (or the state of God's seed) was good when men began to multiply and daughters were born unto them. Note that once again, women are introduced into the equation. What do these daughters of men spiritually represent?

Daughters #1121 a son (as a builder of the family name), in the widest sense (of lit. and fig. relationship)

Daughters #1323 a daughter (used in the same wide sense) (as feminine of #1121)

[Both are from #1129 a primitive root; to build (literal and figurative)]

Born #3205 a primitive root; to bear young, causative to beget; medically, to act as midwife, specifically to show lineage

The *general* spiritual understanding of this verse is that these *daughters* represent those who are unsaved upon the earth. They are spiritually at odds with God's plan for mankind. Many think that these daughters are from Cain's line. And the men are from Adam's line. They have begun marrying outside of that line. But is this true?

Genesis 6:2 "That the sons of God saw the daughters of men that they were fair; and they took them wives of all which they chose."

Sons #1121 a son (as a builder of the family name), in the widest sense (of lit. and fig. relationship…) [from 1129 a primitive root; to build (literal and figurative)]

God #430 plural of [433 a deity or the Deity] gods in the ordinary sense; but specifically used (in the plural thus, especially with the article) of the Supreme God; occasionally applied by way of deference to magistrates; and sometimes as a superlative

Who are these Sons of God? Are these Angels from Heaven as some people teach?

Romans 8:14 "For as many as are led by the Spirit of God, they are the sons of God."

This could apply to both angels and man. We need more information from the Bible.

John 1:12 "But as many as received him, to them gave he power to become the sons of God, even to them that believe on his name:"

Philippians 2:15 "That ye may be blameless and harmless, the sons of God, without rebuke, in the midst of a crooked and perverse nation, among whom ye shine as lights in the world;"

1 John 3:1 "Behold, what manner of love the Father hath bestowed upon us, that we should be called the sons of God: therefore the world knoweth us not, because it knew him not."

These verses should answer the question as to who are the sons of God. And we know that the Spirit of God led these sons of God. (Rom 8:14) The Spirit of God also led these sons of God in Genesis. They were the *Apostles* of that day. In this chapter of Genesis, a huge spiritual battle is taking place at this time. (127) Earth which represents the seed of God verses (776) earth which represents the seed of Satan. The serpent wanted to turn this (127) earth into (776) earth. And he would use the daughters of men to do it.

Like he did to King Solomon. And Samson. And Adam. Anybody remember Job's wife?

Genesis 6:2 "That the sons of God saw the daughters of men that they were fair; and they took them wives of all which they chose."

Fair #2896 good (as an adj.) in the widest sense; used likewise as a noun, both in the masculine and the feminine, the singular and the plural; also as an adverb (well) [from 2895 a primitive root, to be (transitive do or make) good (or well) in the widest sense]

Took #3947 a primitive root; to take (in the widest variety of applications)

Wives #802 a woman (used in the same wide sense as 582 properly a mortal) [feminine of 582 or (376 a man as an individual or a male person)]

The sons of God saw that the daughters were *fair.* I've heard this taught that in the physical sense, the daughters of men were gorgeous, stunning, like beauty contestants. The sons of God had no resistance to their charms. But we know that the sons of God are His representatives on earth, so we should consider the spiritual teaching of these verses. The spiritual state of these "sons of God" was slipping. Soon after these marriages, God declares that He will destroy the earth. The discernment of these sons of God told them that the daughters of men were in line with God's Will. They were not. So these sons of God "took them wives of all which they chose." King Solomon did this. Then again, so did Samson. Their destruction followed these relationships shortly afterward.

Matthew 24:37-39 "But as the days of Noe were, so shall also the coming of the Son of man be. For as in the days that were before the flood they were eating and drinking, marrying and giving in marriage, until the day that Noe entered into the ark, And knew not until the flood came, and took them all away; so shall also the coming of the Son of man be."

When Christ returns they will be marrying and giving in marriage. Just like here. The "sons of God" of today will be "marrying and giving in marriage." Their spiritual state will be just like these men in Genesis. The common denominator is the daughters of men.

Genesis 3:17 "And unto Adam he said, Because thou hast hearkened unto the voice of thy wife, and hast eaten of the tree, of which I commanded thee, saying, Thou shalt not eat of it: cursed is the ground (#127) for thy sake; in sorrow shalt thou eat of it all the days of thy life;"

Adam, the original "son of God" hearkened unto the voice of his wife.

Nehemiah 13:26-27 "Did not Solomon king of Israel sin by these things? yet among many nations was there no king like him, who was beloved of his God, and God made him king over all Israel: nevertheless even him did outlandish women cause to sin. Shall we then hearken unto you to do all this great evil, to transgress against our God in marrying strange wives?"

Do you notice a pattern forming here? You don't? Here are some more…

Numbers 31:15-16 "And Moses said unto them, Have ye saved all the women alive? Behold, these caused the children of Israel, through the counsel of Balaam, to commit trespass against the LORD in the matter of Peor, and there was a plague among the congregation of the LORD."

1 Samuel 2:22-24 "Now Eli was very old, and heard all that his sons did unto all Israel; and how they lay with the women that assembled at the door of the tabernacle of the congregation. And he said unto them, Why do ye such things? for I hear of your evil dealings by all this people. Nay, my sons; for it is no good report that I hear: ye make the LORD'S people to transgress."

And finally one from the Prophet Isaiah.

Isaiah 3:12 "As for my people, children are their oppressors, and women rule over them. O my people, they which lead thee cause thee to err, and destroy the way of thy paths."

This is not something new. This is a pattern we can see all through the Bible. So these sons of God marry the daughters of men because they were fair. And according to the Bible, these acts of the sons of God bring about a huge *reaction* from the LORD.

Genesis 6:3 "And the LORD said, My spirit shall not always strive with man, for that he also is flesh: yet his days shall be an hundred and twenty years."

Spirit #7307 wind; by resemblance breath, i.e. a sensible (or even violent) exhalation; fig. life, anger, un-substantiality…[from 7306 to blow, breathe, to smell, to perceive, enjoy]

Always #5769 [Old] properly concealed, i.e. the vanishing point; generally time out of mind (past or future), i.e. (practically) eternity; freq. adv. (espec. with prep. pref.) always

Strive #1777 a primitive root; to rule; by implication to judge (as umpire); also to strive (as at law) [comparison 113 to rule; sovereign, i.e. controller (human or divine)]

Flesh #1320 flesh (from its freshness); by extension body, person; also (by euphemism) the pudenda of a man [from 1319 to be fresh, i.e. full (rosy, cheerful) to announce]

God's Spirit will not always strive (or rule or judge) with man, "for that he is also flesh." His Spirit ruled and judged mankind through these "sons of God." If something were to interfere with this service for God, Satan could lead many astray. This would be disastrous to those who depended upon these men for spiritual direction.

"Yet his days shall be 120 years." What does this mean? Is it a limit on the lifespan of men and women from here on out? It cannot be. Abraham, Isaac, and Jacob all lived over 120 years. All were born after the deluge. Is this teaching that in 120 years God will destroy the earth with a flood? And that Noah was given 120 years (as a son of God) to preach a warning to the people? I believe that is the teaching here, and that 1 Peter 3 also teaches this.

1 Peter 3:19-20 "By which also he went and preached unto the spirits in prison; Which sometime were disobedient, when once the longsuffering of God waited in the days of Noah, while the ark was a preparing, wherein few, that is, eight souls were saved by water."

Whenever the number of 120 comes up in the Bible, it is a sign that huge changes are in view for that current situation. More details of this can be found in the chapter on King Solomon. As we will read in Genesis 6:7, God states He will destroy man because it "repenteth" him that He had made them. But here, the 120 years is declared because of these unions between the sons of God and the daughters of men. Consider this: these Matthew 24:37-39 verses are a sign to us of Christ's Coming. It references the Genesis flood. Could we apply the 120 years in Genesis to us as a sign also? As a 120 year Tribulation time period? Just wondering...

Genesis 6:4a "There were giants in the earth (#776) in those days; and also after that, when the sons of God came in unto the daughters of men, and they bare children to them,"

Giants #5303 properly a feller, i.e. a bully or tyrant [from 5307 a primitive root; to fall]

Earth #776 from an unused root probable meaning to be firm; the earth (at large, or partitively a land)

Here God uses the word (776) earth and talks about the *giants* of those days. God labels this group of people by using the (776) earth. So who are these giants? Are they angels who get the daughters of men pregnant? Well, we know that the sons of God are not angels. And that God has decreed that everything is created "after its kind." In other words; whatever the species is can only reproduce the same type of species. An angel and a woman cannot produce an offspring because it would not be created after its kind. Also, it is God who gives life to His creation. To permit life to come into being by a angel/woman reproductive act would mean that God would go against His own decree that life is created after its kind. Which He Himself so declared. So, who are these giants? Are they just really tall people? When looking at the context here in these verses, this type of information would seem to be out of place here, although I believe God uses the word giants here to focus us on something other than the height of a person. Our focus on these verses of Genesis has been on the sons of God. From verse 1 to verse 5 we read of the fall of all of the sons of God (save Noah).When the sons of God fall, everyone is led astray from the truth. These giants were prominent during the time of the fall of these sons of God and continued to be until the flood. They are mentioned here because of the wickedness in the earth. As the sons of God were down to their last faithful man (Noah), their replacements as the inspirational leaders (these giants) were running the show. In this verse we read that at this time, the sons of God and the daughters of men are one flesh. And they begin to bare children.

Genesis 6:4b "the same became mighty men which were of old, men of renown."

Mighty #1368 powerful; by implication warrior, tyrant [from the same as 1397 properly a valiant man or warrior; generally a person simply]

Men #582 properly a mortal; hence, a man in general (singular or collective) [from 605 a primitive root; to be frail, feeble, or (figuratively) melancholy]

Old #5769 [Always] properly concealed, i.e. the vanishing point; generally time out of mind (past or future), i.e. (practically) eternity; freq. adv. (espec. with prep. pref.) always

Renown #8034 a primitive word; an appellation, as a mark or memorial of individuality; by implication honor, authority, character

What is important to know here is that the state of mankind at this time was so wicked that all of these "mighty men" or (heroes) were serving the evil one. I wished the Bible had shown us who these men of renown were. Well, here's a thought. We might find this information in Chapter 4 of Genesis. It is interesting that in this chapter we read about the line of Cain. And his line ends (at the flood) with children of renown. Can this Lamech be one of these "sons of God?" Who came in unto daughters of men? (Adah and Zillah) who bare children to him (Jabal; Jubal; Tubal-cain) who became mighty men of renown? (Father of the harp & organ and an instructor of every artificer in brass & iron) It is interesting that these facts about Lamech's family are recorded in Scripture. We are given information about women and famous children here. And they seem to fit the description of these mighty men in this verse of Genesis.

Genesis 6:5a "And GOD saw that the wickedness of man was great in the earth, (#776)"

This means that men like Methuselah (969 years old), and Lamech (777) lived in these times, (During these 120 years) along with these sons of God. Again, it's possible that these men (Methuselah & Lamech) were in fact "sons of God". Both Patriarchal men died right before the flood. We are not told that they walked with God as Noah did. God now uses the (#776) earth to describe the spiritual state of mankind. Before Noah is told to build the Ark, we read:

Genesis 6:12 "And God looked upon the earth (#776), and, behold, it was corrupt; for all flesh had corrupted his way upon the earth. (#776)"

ALL flesh had corrupted his way. God is speaking about men like Methuselah and Lamech (and Noah). ALL of the "flesh" had corrupted, but the spirit of these "sons of God" did not. (Remember, Scripture tells us that Noah walked with God.) Here we are shown that a "son of God" can have the spirit of God and still have corrupted flesh.

Genesis 6:5b "and that every imagination of the thoughts of his heart was only evil continually."

And every #3605 the Whole; hence, all, any or every (in the singular only, but often in a plural sense) [from 3634 (PR) to complete]

Imagination #3336 a form; fig. conception (i.e. purpose) [from 3335 to mould into a form; especially as a potter; fig. to determine (i.e. form a resolution)]

Thoughts #4284 a contrivance, i.e. (concretely) a texture, machine, or (abstractly) intention, plan (whether bed, a plot, or good, advice) [from 2803 (PR) to Plait or interpenetrate, i.e. (lit) weave or (generally) to fabricate]

Heart #3820 the Heart; also used (fig) very widely for the feelings, the will and even the intellect; likewise for the center of anything [a form of 3824 the heart (as the most interior organ)]

Only #7535 the same as [7534 emaciated (as if flattened out)] as a noun; properly leanness, i.e. (fig) limitation; only adv. merely, or (conjunction) although

Evil #7451 Bad or (as noun) Evil (naturally or morally) [from 7489 (PR) to spoil (lit. by breaking to pieces); (fig. to make or be good for nothing); bad]

Continually #3117 from an unused root meaning: to be Hot; a Day (as the warm hours), whether lit. (from sunrise to sunset, or from one sunset to the next), or fig. (a space of time defined by an associated term), [often used adverbially]

This is one of the most frightening statements about mankind from the Bible. Frightening because this will also be the state of mankind's heart when Jesus returns in the clouds. To try to understand what this is teaching we must break this down. We know right off the bat that everything that was coming out of the heart was evil everyday or (day to day). And this evil was coming out through the thoughts of a person's heart. Thoughts' being the passageway or channel mankind uses to bring sin into existence. These thoughts served the self and not God. They became imagination or *sin* in God's eyes. This is a pattern in mankind that continues to this day. Scripture teaches of our *spiritual state* in the Bible. In Jeremiah, God speaks of those He led out of Egypt and out of bondage.

Jeremiah 7:24 "But they hearkened not, nor inclined their ear, but walked in the counsels and in the imagination of their evil heart, and went backward, and not forward."

As the Fathers *walked* in Jeremiah chapter 7, so now do the sons in chapter 16.

Jeremiah 16:11-12 "Then shalt thou say unto them, Because your fathers have forsaken me, saith the LORD, and have walked after other gods, and have served them, and have worshipped them, and have forsaken me, and have not kept my law; And ye have done worse than your fathers; for, behold, ye walk every one after the imagination of his evil heart, that they may not hearken unto me:"

Do you notice a pattern in this language? God speaks of the evil heart of man.

Jeremiah 17:9 "The heart is deceitful above all things, and desperately wicked: who can know it?"

Only God can (see Jeremiah 17:10). So the state of the (776) earth was very wicked. It will be the same when Christ returns. We ask ourselves, will Christ *feel* toward mankind the same way as He did in the next verse of Genesis?

Genesis 6:6 "And it repented the LORD that he had made man (#120) on the earth (#776), and it grieved him at his heart."

Repented #5162 a primitive root; properly to sigh, i.e. breathe strongly; by implication to be sorry, i.e. (in a favorable sense) to pity, console or (reflexively) rue; or (unfavorably) to avenge (oneself)

Grieved #6087 a primitive root; properly to carve, i.e. fabricate or fashion; hence, (in a bad sense) to worry, pain or anger

The LORD was grieved at His Heart. Mankind no longer loved nor served their God.

Mark 3:4-5 "And he saith unto them, Is it lawful to do good on the sabbath days, or to do evil? to save life, or to kill? But they held their peace. And when he had looked round about on them with anger, being grieved for the hardness of their hearts, he saith unto the man, Stretch forth thine hand. And he stretched it out: and his hand was restored whole as the other."

Jesus was grieved at those religious rulers in the Synagogue. (because of the hardness of their hearts) These Pharisees no longer loved nor served their God.

Ephesians 4:30 "And grieve not the holy Spirit of God, whereby ye are sealed unto the day of redemption."

Grieve #3076 to distress; reflexively or passively to be sad [from 3077 sadness]

As with the LORD and Jesus Christ, we are told by Scripture that we can also grieve the Holy Spirit. What does this tell us about our Heavenly Father? That He loves us? Please notice that after the LORD was grieved with mankind, He destroyed them with a flood. And take note what Jesus eventually prophesied for these Pharisees and Sadducees. (The Lake of Fire) What kind of reaction should we expect from grieving the Holy Spirit? We are told in the book of 1 Corinthians where Paul speaks to the Brethren at Corinth.

1 Corinthians 3:15-17 "If any man's work shall be burned, he shall suffer loss: but he himself shall be saved; yet so as by fire. Know ye not that ye are the temple of God, and that the Spirit of God dwelleth in you? If any man defile the temple of God, him shall God destroy; for the temple of God is holy, which temple ye are."

My advice is that we should not grieve the Holy Spirit. The keyword here is *destroy*. God can destroy a person in many ways and at any time. Heed this warning.

Genesis 6:7 "And the LORD said, I will destroy man whom I have created from the face of the earth (#127); both man, and beast, and the creeping thing, and the fowls of the air; for it repenteth me that I have made them."

It repented the LORD that he made man (male and female). God did not repent over making man in His Image, but over creating *male & female* from this man. So, He will destroy man (a son of God) from the *face* of the (127) Earth (soil). The male and the female, the creeping thing, and the fowls of the air. Complete destruction of the beings that have the breath of life. God repeats that He repents that He made them. But one man of God (a son of God) finds grace. He will not be destroyed.

Genesis 6:8 "But Noah found grace in the eyes of the LORD."

And so Noah and his sons and their wives were spared from the destruction of the flood to come. Noah is told to build an ark to contain everything that God wanted to save.

Genesis 6:22 "Thus did Noah; according to all that God commanded him, so did he."

Many believe that the return of Christ is not far off. Many preach that this generation (our generation) has a very good chance of witnessing this. That would mean that the heart of man today must be as the heart of these people here in Genesis.

Genesis 6:5 "And GOD saw that the wickedness of man was great in the earth, and that every imagination of the thoughts of his heart was only evil continually."

The thoughts of the heart are only evil continually. This is God's assessment of us. We must look at this from the bigger picture. We are here to experience God's Salvation plan. All of us (to various degrees) are given enough knowledge of the LORD to be held responsible for our actions that relate to this. To reject God's Spirit to lead us and instead put our own spirit in charge, assures us that every imagination of our heart will be only evil continually. This comes with a heavy price. One more comment on the daughters of men before we go. We read in Genesis chapter 9.

Genesis 9:8-9 "And God spake unto Noah, and to his sons with him, saying, And I, behold, I establish my <u>covenant</u> with you, and with your seed after you;"

Covenant #1285 [from 1262 to select, to feed, to render clear (in the sense of cutting-like 1254 to cut down) a compact (because made by passing between pieces of flesh)

Seed #2233 seed; fig. fruit, plant, sowing-time, posterity [from 2232 to sow; fig. to disseminate, plant, fructify]

Please note that this covenant is made between Noah and his sons. When we look at the word seed, we easily can apply this spiritually. They are to produce *fruit*, which is they are to produce a people that worship their God. This is what the sons of God were to do. I believe that Shem, Ham, & Japheth were in fact, sons of God. The very same sons of God who married the daughters of men.

Genesis 9:19 "These are the three sons of Noah: and of them was the whole earth overspread."

Miriam The Prophetess

"To me Miriam the Prophetess is a classic example of a tare (an unsaved person) in the Church. She claimed spiritual authority that was not hers. She acted upon this belief in front of God and Israel. This reminded me of Eve in the Garden of Eden. The life of Miriam also illustrates the spiritual limitations that are placed upon the woman."

Imagine my surprise when I heard gasps of air and looks of disbelief when I shared my thoughts on Miriam the *prophetess* with my Bible study group. "What? How could you even think of such a thing? Isn't she a Prophetess? Doesn't that mean she is saved?"

Miriam #4813 Rebelliously; Mirjam [from 4805 bitterness, i.e. rebellion; concr. bitter]

Prophetess #5031 a prophetess or (gen.) inspired woman; by implication a poetess; by association a prophet's wife [feminine of 5030 a prophet or (gen.) inspired man]

Most do not know what the name of Miriam means. When they look it up they are puzzled by the definition found there. (Rebelliously from the word bitterness.)

Deuteronomy 24:8-9 "Take heed in the plague of leprosy, that thou observe diligently, and do

according to all that the priests the Levites shall teach you: as I commanded them, so ye shall observe to do. Remember what the LORD thy God did unto Miriam by the way, after that ye were come forth out of Egypt."

In Deuteronomy chapter 24, Moses relays the laws and ordinances that God commands from all of Israel. Why would Moses remind Israel what the LORD did to Miriam? We find that answer in the Book of Numbers.

Numbers 12:1-2 "And Miriam and Aaron spake against Moses because of the Ethiopian woman whom he had married: for he had married an Ethiopian woman. And they said, Hath the LORD indeed spoken only by Moses? hath he not spoken also by us? And the LORD heard it."

The Ethiopian woman mentioned here is commonly taught as Zipporah the daughter of Reuel (who is also known as Jethro and Raguel) the priest of Midian. You find this in Exodus chapter two. As we read through Numbers 12, we find that this marriage to the Ethiopian woman is not the focus of this chapter. Miriam and Aaron need a reason to bring Moses down a level so the people of Israel would listen to them. They follow up this propaganda by claiming that the LORD speaks through them as He has with Moses. This speech of theirs gets the God's attention. "And the LORD heard it."

Numbers 12:3 "(Now the man Moses was very meek, above all the men which were upon the face of the earth.)"

Moses #4872 drawing out (of the water), i.e. rescued; Mosheh, the Israelite lawgiver [from 4871 a primitive root; to pull out (lit or fig)]

Meek #6035 depressed (fig.), in mind (gentle) or circumstances (needy, especially saintly) [from 6031 a primitive root to depress (in various applications)]

Earth #127 soil (from its general redness) [from 119 to show blood (in the face)]

Here we have pleura of information about the man Moses. His name means rescued. He was (drawn out) of the water. His meekness is compared to all of the men on the face of the #127 earth. (Not the #776 earth.) Moses spiritual standing with God is expressed to us by all of the wordage utilized here. He is a true servant of God. Note that as Aaron and Miriam are chastising Moses, we do not read about any response from him. Instead, God comes to his defense.

Numbers 12:4-5 "And the LORD spake suddenly unto Moses, and unto Aaron, and unto Miriam, Come out ye three unto the tabernacle of the congregation. And they three came out. And the LORD came down in the pillar of the cloud, and stood in the door of the tabernacle, and called Aaron and Miriam: and they both came forth."

Aaron #175 of uncertain derivation; Aharon, the brother of Moses

Miriam #4813 Rebelliously; Mirjam [from 4805 bitterness, i.e. rebellion; concr. bitter]

Why is God angry against Aaron & Miriam? Is it because they are criticizing Moses for marrying an Ethiopian woman? Or is it their claim of a *Prophet* status?

Numbers 12:6 "And he said, Hear now my words: If there be a prophet among you, I the LORD will make myself known unto him in a vision, and will speak unto him in a dream."

Prophet #5030 a prophet or (gen.) inspired man [from 5012 a primitive root; to prophesy, i.e. speak (or sing) by inspiration (in prediction or simple discourse)]

Vision #4758 a view (the act of seeing); also an appearance (the thing seen), whether (real) a shape (especially if handsome, comeliness; often plural the looks) or (mentally) a vision [from 7200 a primitive root; to see lit. or fig. (in numerous applications)]

Dream #2472 a dream [from 2492 a primitive root; properly to bind firmly, i.e. (by implication) to be (causative to make) plump; also (through the figurative sense of dumbness) to dream]

We find that God does not even mention the issue of the Ethiopian wife. Instead, the LORD comments on who is His prophet and how they will know it. Compare this verse to what we find in the Book of Acts.

Acts 2:17 "And it shall come to pass in the last days, saith God, I will pour out of my Spirit upon all flesh: and your sons and your daughters shall prophesy, and your young men shall see visions, and your old men shall dream dreams:"

Note that it is to the men here (young and old) who will receive a dream or a vision.

God states that He will make Himself known to the prophet, and because He is the same today as yesterday and tomorrow, this communication must be to a man. This is part of the *example* God teaches to Israel in the Deuteronomy verses. We know that Aaron was a prophet of God. And the LORD spoke to the people using Aaron's mouth.

Exodus 7:1 "And the LORD said unto Moses, See, I have made thee a god to Pharaoh: and Aaron thy brother shall be thy prophet."

Exodus 4:15-16 "And thou shalt speak unto him, and put words in his mouth: and I will be with thy mouth, and with his mouth, and will teach you what ye shall do. And he shall be thy spokesman unto the people: and he shall be, even he shall be to thee instead of a mouth, and thou shalt be to him instead of God."

So Aaron *qualifies* as a prophet of God. Miriam does not. But wait a minute; isn't she called a Prophetess in Exodus chapter 15? I'll address that shortly. God continues.

Numbers 12:7-8 "My servant Moses is not so, who is faithful in all mine house. With him will I speak mouth to mouth, even apparently, and not in dark speeches; and the similitude of the LORD shall he behold: wherefore then were ye not afraid to speak against my servant Moses?"

Dark #2420 Speeches #2420

A puzzle, hence, a trick, conundrum, sententious maxim [from 2330 a primitive root; properly to tie a knot, i.e. (fig) to propound a riddle]

Moses is a very special servant of God. Meek above all the men on the face of the earth and "faithful in all mine house." God speaks to Moses "mouth to mouth" or clearly. He understands

God's Will without confusion. Wherefore, God asks Aaron and Miriam, why are you not afraid when speaking up against My Servant? Both of them had forgotten the spiritual authority here. This is another part of that *example* we read about in Deuteronomy. First God spells this out to Aaron and Miriam. And then He applies the appropriate punishment to those who earned it.

Numbers 12:9-10 "And the anger of the LORD was kindled against them; and he departed. And the cloud departed from off the tabernacle; and, behold, Miriam became leprous, white as snow: and Aaron looked upon Miriam, and, behold, she was leprous."

Leprous #6879 a primitive root; to scourge, i.e. (intr. and fig.) to be stricken with leprosy

Here is the question that everyone asks. Why does God only strike Miriam with leprosy? Why didn't Aaron receive this disease as well? First of all, Aaron is a prophet of the LORD and Miriam is not. The focus here is on who speaks for God and the authority given to Moses. The marriage to the Ethiopian woman is not mentioned at all. God then creates a dire situation in the lives of these three. To deal with this, they must follow God's order of spiritual authority. Miriam (the woman) needs someone who has the spiritual authority (the man) Aaron to intercede for her. Miriam is now *silent in the church.*

Numbers 12:11-12 "And Aaron said unto Moses, Alas, my lord, I beseech thee, lay not the sin upon us, wherein we have done foolishly, and wherein we have sinned. Let her not be as one dead, of whom the flesh is half consumed when he cometh out of his mother's womb."

Sin #2403 an offence (sometimes habitual sinfulness), and its penalty, occasion, sacrifice, or expiation; also (concretely) an offender [from 2398 a primitive root; to miss; hence, (fig, and gen.) to sin; by infer. to forfeit, lack, expiate, repent, (causative) lead astray, condemn]

Aaron who now fully recognizes his position in this order of authority goes through the appropriate channels to help his sister Miriam. He confesses both of their sin to Moses and pleads "my lord" (a picture of Jesus Christ on earth), to forgive them. Only after this does he ask for the healing of their sister Miriam.

Numbers 12:13-16 "And Moses cried unto the LORD, saying, Heal her now, O God, I beseech thee. And the LORD said unto Moses, If her father had but spit in her face, should she not be ashamed seven days? let her be shut out from the camp seven days, and after that let her be received in again. And Miriam was shut out from the camp seven days: and the people journeyed not till Miriam was brought in again. And afterward the people removed from Hazeroth, and pitched in the wilderness of Paran."

Moses pleads to the LORD for her immediate healing. God imposes a sentence of 7 days of being shut outside of the camp for Miriam. We are not sure that Miriam was healed right away. She may have been cured after spending seven days outside the camp. We do not read about her after this incident. I believe that this punishment devastated Miriam. Her death is recorded in the first verse of Numbers chapter 20.

Did you know that these three are mentioned together in another book of the Bible? It comes with the same warning to the children of Israel. We find this in the book of Micah.

Micah 6:3-4 "O my people, what have I done unto thee? and wherein have I wearied thee? testify against me. For I brought thee up out of the land of Egypt, and redeemed thee out of the house of servants; and I sent before thee Moses, Aaron, and Miriam."

Moses #4872 drawing out (of the water), i.e. rescued; Mosheh, the Israelite lawgiver [from 4871 a primitive root; to pull out (lit or fig)]

Aaron #175 of uncertain derivation; Aharon, the brother of Moses

Miriam #4813 Rebelliously; Mirjam [from 4805 bitterness, i.e. rebellion; concr. bitter]

God reminds the people of this incident of leprosy in the camp. And how they ignored the spiritual authority given to them from the LORD. But I don't think that the leprosy given to Miriam was the only judgment concerning her. Let's look closer at the life of Miriam.

Numbers 26:59 "And the name of Amram's wife was Jochebed, the daughter of Levi, whom her mother bare to Levi in Egypt: and she bare unto Amram Aaron and Moses, and Miriam their sister."

Amram and Jochebed name their daughter Mirjam. A name associated with rebelling and bitterness. There is always a reason for a person's name in the Bible. It generally gives the reader a clue as to that person's *spiritual* standing with God. Not always, but generally. This does not bode well for their sister. We next find Miriam spying on her little brother as he is placed in the river in an ark of bulrushes.

Exodus 2:4-9 "And his sister stood afar off, to wit what would be done to him. And the daughter of Pharaoh came down to wash herself at the river; and her maidens walked along by the river's side; and when she saw the ark among the flags, she sent her maid to fetch it. And when she had opened it, she saw the child: and, behold, the babe wept. And she had compassion on him, and said, This is one of the Hebrews' children. Then said his sister to Pharaoh's daughter, Shall I go and call to thee a nurse of the Hebrew women, that she may nurse the child for thee? And Pharaoh's daughter said to her, Go. And the maid went and called the child's mother. And Pharaoh's daughter said unto her, Take this child away, and nurse it for me, and I will give thee thy wages. And the woman took the child, and nursed it."

This worked out well for Moses and his mother. Miriam was at the right place at the right time. Or was she? No doubt that God used her here, but no child of mine should be that close to the Pharaoh's daughter. She shows a recklessness here that we will see in her adult life. We read about her again in the 15th book of Exodus. The children of Israel have just passed through the Red Sea. They sing the song of Moses in the first 19 verses of Exodus 15, thanking the LORD and giving Him the Glory for saving them.

Exodus 15:20-23 "And Miriam the prophetess, the sister of Aaron, took a timbrel in her hand; and all the women went out after her with timbrels and with dances. And Miriam answered them, Sing ye to the LORD, for he hath triumphed gloriously; the horse and his rider hath he thrown into the sea. So

Moses brought Israel from the Red sea, and they went out into the wilderness of Shur; and they went three days in the wilderness, and found no water. And when they came to Marah, they could not drink of the waters of Marah, for they were bitter: therefore the name of it was called Marah."

There are two points to be considered here. The first is why is she called Miriam the prophetess?

Miriam #4813 Rebelliously; Mirjam [from 4805 bitterness, i.e. rebellion; concr. bitter]

Prophetess #5031 a prophetess or (gen.) inspired woman; by implication a poetess; by association a prophet's wife [feminine of 5030 a prophet or (gen.) inspired man]

The rebellious inspired woman. That doesn't sound good. Maybe she is a prophetess by association. (I think that this is the case. Note that the verse continues "the sister of Aaron.") And I read nowhere in the Bible about Miriam being *inspired* to say anything to the people from the LORD. Maybe they are referring to this account in Exodus? Maybe Miriam is inspired by the LORD here and leads the women to sing praises? It is interesting that she changes the first couple of words in the song. "I will sing unto the LORD" (verse 1) becomes "Sing ye to the LORD" (verse 21). The second point is that 3 days later as they were searching for water, they come across the waters of Marah.

Marah #4785 bitter; Marah, a place in the desert [the same as 4751 feminine; bitter (lit. or fig.); also (as noun) bitterness, or (adv.) bitterly]

Isn't this interesting? Is it telling us something about Miriam? Again she is brash in her actions. I believe that the LORD was displeased with her actions (and the women.) Lets look at another example of women singing praises in the Bible.

1 Samuel 18:6-9 "And it came to pass as they came, when David was returned from the slaughter of the Philistine, that the women came out of all cities of Israel, singing and dancing, to meet king Saul, with tabrets, with joy, and with instruments of musick. And the women answered one another as they played, and said, Saul hath slain his thousands, and David his ten thousands. And Saul was very wroth, and the saying displeased him; and he said, They have ascribed unto David ten thousands, and to me they have ascribed but thousands: and what can he have more but the kingdom? And Saul eyed David from that day and forward."

Dire results resulting from praise. Both of these examples brought chastisement upon the people of Israel. That brings us up to the incident in the Book of Numbers chapter 12.

Deuteronomy 24:8-9 "Take heed in the plague of leprosy, that thou observe diligently, and do according to all that the priests the Levites shall teach you: as I commanded them, so ye shall observe to do. Remember what the LORD thy God did unto Miriam by the way, after that ye were come forth out of Egypt."

"Remember what the LORD thy God did unto Miriam by the way." This reminder also includes where they buried her when she died. Lets compare burial places for the three.

Deuteronomy 34:1 "And Moses went up from the plains of Moab unto the mountain of Nebo, to the top of Pisgah, that is over against Jericho. And the LORD shewed him all the land of Gilead, unto Dan,"

Deuteronomy 34:5-8 "So Moses the servant of the LORD died there in the land of Moab, according to the word of the LORD. And he buried him in a valley in the land of Moab, over against Bethpeor: but no man knoweth of his sepulchre unto this day. And Moses was an hundred and twenty years old when he died: his eye was not dim, nor his natural force abated. And the children of Israel wept for Moses in the plains of Moab thirty days: so the days of weeping and mourning for Moses were ended."

In the mountain they bury Moses. Now we look at Aaron.

Numbers 33:38-39 "And Aaron the priest went up into mount Hor at the commandment of the LORD, and died there, in the fortieth year after the children of Israel were come out of the land of Egypt, in the first day of the fifth month. And Aaron was an hundred and twenty and three years old when he died in mount Hor."

In the mountain they bury Aaron. And now we look at the death of Miriam.

Numbers 20:1 "Then came the children of Israel, even the whole congregation, into the desert of Zin in the first month: and the people abode in Kadesh; and Miriam died there, and was buried there."

Zin #6790 from an unused root meaning to prick; a crag; Tsin, a part of the desert.

Kadesh #6946 sanctuary [the same as 6945 a (quasi) sacred person, i.e. (tech.) a (male) devotee (by prostitution) to licentious idolatry]

In the desert of Zin, in Kadesh, they bury Miriam the Prophetess. This is what happens to those who *rebel* against the LORD. To those who profess a spiritual authority that was never given to them.

The Vow Of A Woman

In this chapter of Numbers we find that making a vow to the LORD is different for the man and the woman. Not only does his clearly reflect the cursed *spiritual* state of the woman, but illustrates the responsibility given to the man to be a covering.

Numbers 30:1 "And Moses spake unto the heads of the tribes concerning the children of Israel, saying, This is the thing which the LORD hath commanded."

Commanded #6680 a primitive root; (intensively) to constitute, enjoin

This thing that the LORD commands, must be obeyed without question.

Numbers 30:2 "If a man vow a vow unto the LORD, or swear an oath to bind his soul with a bond; he shall not break his word, he shall do according to all that proceedeth out of his mouth."

Vow #5087 [#5088] a primitive root; to promise (positive to do or give something to God) #5088 a promise (to God); also (concretely) a thing promised [from 5087]

Oath #7621 properly something sworn, i.e. an oath [feminine passive participle of 7650-a primitive root; property to be complete, but used only as a denomination from 7651; to seven oneself, i.e. swear (as if by repeating a declaration seven times)]

Bind #631 a primitive root; to yoke or hitch; by anal. to fasten in any sense, to join battle

Bond #632 an obligation or vow (of abstinence) [from 631]

Even today, it is important to understand the teaching here. This involves the soul as well as the flesh. First of all, what is this vow? Is it someone dedicating his or her self to a lifetime of Gods service? Or is it just saying "God, if you do this one thing for me, I promise I will go to Church next Sunday." These both are promises made that place that person's soul in a debt situation. Personal vows and oaths can cover a myriad of subjects. Our focus here is on how these vows are applied to the man and to the woman. Let's look closer at what this verse is saying. We can see that our vow is to God. And each man is personally responsible for the oath he makes. There is no mediator between him and the LORD. Primarily, this vow is spoken. (The chapter highlights words like uttered and heard.) And that each man is held accountable to what he has vowed. His soul is bound by this oath; he is not to break his promise.

Ecclesiastes 5:4-6 "When thou vowest a vow unto God, defer not to pay it; for he hath no pleasure in fools: pay that which thou hast vowed. Better is it that thou shouldest not vow, than that thou shouldest vow and not pay. Suffer not thy mouth to cause thy flesh to sin; neither say thou before the angel, that it was an error: wherefore should God be angry at thy voice, and destroy the work of thine hands?"

He will destroy the works of "thine hands." This could be your heavenly as well as your earthly *treasures*. God has no pleasure in fools. There will come a time that the LORD will collect all that is promised Him.

Psalm 50:14 "Offer unto God thanksgiving; and pay thy vows unto the most High:"

We will also find warnings in Deuteronomy chapter 23. In addition when a soul made an oath to God, there was a sacrifice expected from the one who made it.

Leviticus 22:18-19 "Speak unto Aaron, and to his sons, and unto all the children of Israel, and say unto them, Whatsoever he be of the house of Israel, or of the strangers in Israel, that will offer his oblation for all his vows, and for all his freewill offerings, which they will offer unto the LORD for a burnt offering; Ye shall offer at your own will a male without blemish, of the beeves, of the sheep, or of the goats."

A Nazarite vow included an additional *sacrifice* of separating themselves from wine & strong drink, all forms of grapes, and so on. (Numbers chapter 6) This is why there is a general belief in that when you ask God for a favor, there is something expected back from you. Some form of sacrifice. He is very serious about vows. And we should be to.

Numbers 30:3 " If a woman also vow a vow unto the LORD, and bind herself by a bond, being in her father's house in her youth;"

Now we look at a woman's vow to God. The woman makes a (spoken) vow just as the man does. This verse talks about a young girl or maid (an unmarried woman).

Numbers 30:4-5 "And her father hear her vow, and her bond wherewith she hath bound her soul, and her father shall hold his peace at her: then all her vows shall stand, and every bond wherewith she hath bound her soul shall stand. But if her father disallow her in the day that he heareth; not any of her vows, or of her bonds wherewith she hath bound her soul, shall stand: and the LORD shall forgive her, because her father disallowed her."

Peace #2790 a primitive root; to scratch, i.e. (by implication) to engrave, plow,; hence, (from the use of tools) to fabricate (of any material); fig. to devise (in a bad sense); hence, (from the idea of secrecy) to be silent, to let alone; hence, (by implication) to be deaf (as an accompaniment of dumbness)

Disallow (ed) #5106 a primitive root; to refuse, forbid, dissuade, or neutralize

Forgive #5545 a primitive root; to forgive

The father has the right to approve or disapprove of his daughter's vows to God. This is astounding information. A father must have the spiritual authority over his daughter in order to do this. Think of this. A young woman from her heart speaks a vow to serve or promise something to Almighty God. And we know that if the father says nothing to refute his daughter's vow, the vow stands. That in itself is very serious, as the Bible says that vows are to be kept. But if the father disallows her vow "in the day that he heareth", the *responsibility* of that vow is not applied to her. Please note that there are no special instructions for a male son here. This gives us further proof of the spiritual roles and responsibilities (via the curse) given to the man and the woman in the Garden of Eden. But this is for a young woman. What about a woman who marries?

Numbers 30:6-8 "And if she had at all an husband, when she vowed, or uttered ought out of her lips, wherewith she bound her soul; And her husband heard it, and held his peace at her in the day that he heard it: then her vows shall stand, and her bonds wherewith she bound her soul shall stand. But if her husband disallowed her on the day that he heard it; then he shall make her vow which she vowed, and that which she uttered with her lips, wherewith she bound her soul, of none effect: and the LORD shall forgive her."

Husband #376 a man as a individual or a male person; often used as an adjunct to a more definite term (and in such cases frequently not expressed in translation)

None #3808 a primitive particle; not (the simple or abstract negation); by implication no, often used with other particles

Effect #6565 a primitive root; to break up (usually fig., i.e. to violate, frustrate)

Now the daughter grows up and takes a husband. She is now in a marriage. As with the previous verses concerning the daughter's vows, we see the same language used here. The difference is the man in the woman's life. The husband has the same authority over the woman's vows as the father had. Therefore the husband must also have some spiritual authority over his wife in order to do this. This authority is given to these men from God. God did not recreate his creation of men and women since these verses were written. Physically and emotionally and spiritually we are the same as these men and women here. We are all created the same and all are under the curses from God in Eden. These verses are a by-product from that. These are instructions that need to be understood and followed even today. In the New Testament there are many verses that place limits on the women in the Church and in the home. These limits relate to *spiritual things.* These deal specifically about her relationship to God. In addition, there are many verses that teach the spiritual condition of the woman. These verses are there for a reason. They are to help us form our relationship to God. But what if a woman's spiritual authority dies or leaves her? Is she *freed* from an old vow she made while he was with her?

Numbers 30:9 "But every vow of a widow, and of her that is divorced, wherewith they have bound their souls, shall stand against her."

Here we read that her old vows still stand. She is still *bound* to them. The death of her husband or a divorce does not alter the condition of her vows. They still apply.

Numbers 30:10-12 "And if she vowed in her husband's house, or bound her soul by a bond with an oath; And her husband heard it, and held his peace at her, and disallowed her not: then all her vows shall stand, and every bond wherewith she bound her soul shall stand. But if her husband hath utterly made them void on the day he heard them; then whatsoever proceeded out of her lips concerning her vows, or concerning the bond of her soul, shall not stand: her husband hath made them void; and the LORD shall forgive her."

Again the language is the same as it was for the daughter and the married woman. The husband who has either died or left (who allowed or disallowed his wife's vows when he heard it) maintains the spiritual authority over her vow. "The LORD shall forgive her", (meaning she can make a vow to God and not keep it.) There will be no punishment from God. If there is a problem regarding the woman's vow, it is the man's problem now. Note that for a man's oath, it is a direct man to God process. For the female vow, we needed to look at every position for her. The unmarried state, the married state, and the divorced or widowed state of the woman. It is very clear how the LORD wants this vow *process* to operate. He sums it up in the next few verses using the same language as before. But this time God uses the word iniquity.

Numbers 30:13-15 "Every vow, and every binding oath to afflict the soul, her husband may establish it, or her husband may make it void. But if her husband altogether hold his peace at her from day to day; then he establisheth all her vows, or all her bonds, which are upon her: he confirmeth them, because he held his peace at her in the day that he heard them. But if he shall any ways make them void after that he hath heard them; then he shall bear her iniquity."

Establisheth [Confirmeth] #6965 a primitive root; to rise (in various applications, lit. fig. intensively and causatively)

Iniquity #5771 perversity, i.e. (moral) evil [from 5753 a primitive root; to crook]

With spiritual authority comes spiritual responsibility. If the husband takes back or makes void a wife's vow or oath that he consented to in the past, then he shall bear her iniquity. God would do this to the man because...

Ephesians 5:23 "For the husband is the head of the wife, even as Christ is the head of the church: and he is the saviour of the body."

The male is the head of the woman. He is also the spiritual covering of the woman. This is taught in 1 Corinthians 11. In order for man to fulfill this role, he was endowed this spiritual ability. And along with this ability came a spiritual responsibility to watch over his household.

1 Corinthians 11:10 "For this cause ought the woman to have power on her head because of the angels."

Because of the covering that was needed for the woman, a male was spiritually necessary all of the time. It is clear in these Numbers verses that the vow of a woman had to have male approval in order for it to stand. This is a direct consequence of how the woman was created and then the curse that God applied to her.

Numbers 30:16 "These are the statutes, which the LORD commanded Moses, between a man and his wife, between the father and his daughter, being yet in her youth in her father's house."

Statutes #2706 an enactment; hence, an appointment (of time, space, quantity, labor or usage) [from 2710 properly to hack, i.e. engrave; by implication to enact (laws being cut in stone or metal tablets in primitive times) or (generally) prescribe]

Spiritual instructions from God are no longer understood nor followed today. Let's look at the marriage vows. When two people get married in a Christian fashion, they both make a vow to God. These are in standard Christian marriage vows. God tells us we are to pay up. Make good the vow. The husband hears his wife's vow during the marriage ceremony and keeps his peace. The vow for the woman stands. The responsibility is upon the woman. But wait! They get a divorce! The husband now takes back the vow.

Numbers 30:15 "But if he shall <u>any ways make them void</u> after that he hath heard them; then he shall bear her iniquity."

He now bears her iniquity. What a mess. God created these rules for our good. Mankind has made a joke of them. Our society reflects our lack of understanding or obedience to His Word. Many souls suffer because we do not want any rules or some authority placed over us. The consequences of not following the Bible's instructions will always bring sorrow to each and every one of us.

Luke 17:26-27 "And as it was in the days of Noe, so shall it be also in the days of the Son of man. They did eat, they drank, they married wives, they were given in marriage, until the day that Noe entered into the ark, and the flood came, and destroyed them all."

And people will still be making vows in their marriages, right up to the day when the Son of man is revealed.

Divorce And Re-Marriage

Because God's marriage institution is very important spiritually as well as physically to mankind, we need to look at how a divorce impacts the spiritual headship. The laws for this act are found in the Book of Deuteronomy.

Deuteronomy 24:1-4 "When a man hath taken a wife, and married her, and it come to pass that she find no favour in his eyes, because he hath found some uncleanness in her: then let him write her a bill of divorcement, and give it in her hand, and send her out of his house. And when she is departed out of his house, she may go and be another man's wife. And if the latter husband hate her, and write her a bill of divorcement, and giveth it in her hand, and sendeth her out of his house; or if the latter husband die, which took her to be his wife; Her former husband, which sent her away, may not take her again to be his wife, after that she is defiled; for that is abomination before the LORD: and thou shalt not cause the land to sin, which the LORD thy God giveth thee for an inheritance."

Isn't it amazing that one woman can cause such extreme reactions (with possible eternal ramifications) for her and to the men in her life. Don't miss this very important fact in these verses. The power of *attorney* is given to the husband. It is he that has the final say. Now, many people immediately dismiss this type of teaching by believing in a *culture* scenario. That is, the culture of the day is used to interpret the Scriptures given and how they are applied. We read about these Old Testament people and say to ourselves, "Well that was in *their* day, we now live in a completely different culture. The husband has this power because that is the way *they* lived back then. After all, we don't practice animal sacrifices anymore, do we?" This very simple approach dismisses the spiritual order set up by God. These verses as well as many others throughout the Bible (beginning with the creation of mankind and the curse that was placed upon it) are to be understood in its entirely. The scriptures are consistent in their teaching of a spiritual order and how it affects our daily lives. This is constant even of the teaching of sacrifices to God. We are still to offer up our (animal sacrifice) to Him everyday. We are to *die* to ourselves.

Deuteronomy 24:1-2 "When a man hath taken a wife, and married her, and it come to pass that she find no favour in his eyes, because he hath found some uncleanness in her: then let him write her a bill of divorcement, and give it in her hand, and send her out of his house. And when she is departed out of his house, she may go and be another man's wife."

Divorcement #3748 a cutting (of the matrimonial bond), i.e. divorce [from 3772 a primitive root; to cut (off, down or asunder); by implication to destroy or consume]

A written bill of divorcement placed in her hand was what you needed. This would back-up her story that she was divorced. Nobody wanted to be guilty of adultery in Israel.

"She find no favour in his eyes, because he hath found some uncleanness in her"

I have heard many different interpretations of this verse, the most extreme involving the husband catching the wife in the act of adultery (or shortly afterward.) Is this true? A strong argument is made for this because of the verse we read in Matthew chapter 5.

Matthew 5:32 "But I say unto you, That whosoever shall put away his wife, saving for the cause of fornication, causeth her to commit adultery: and whosoever shall marry her that is divorced committeth adultery."

This would mean the teaching of divorcement remained the same. If the woman *cheats* on her marriage, the husband has the option of divorce. There are no rules for the wives to put away the husband. This follows the spiritual order that was set up by God. Today mankind sets up the spiritual order in this world (and enforces it.)

"She find no favour in his eyes, because he hath found some uncleanness in her"

Let's look at this verse again, but this time we will apply a spiritual application.

Favour #2580 graciousness, i.e. **subjectively (kindness, favor)** or objectively (beauty) [from 2603 a primitive root properly to **bend or stoop in kindness to an inferior**; to favor, bestow; causatively to implore (i.e. move to favor by petition)]

Uncleanness #6172 nudity, literally (especially the pudenda) or **figuratively (disgrace, blemish)** [from 6168 a primitive root; to be (causatively make) bare; hence, to empty, pour out, demolish]

The spiritual curse given to the woman in Genesis was that she would desire her husband and he would rule over her. This resulted in the woman being *bound* to her husband as long as he lives. Get the connection? Marriage is a very serious physical business. It is also a serious spiritual business. There are spiritual ramifications to all of the parties who are involved in a marriage or remarriage. God is speaking about a person being *defiled* and that this is an abomination. The act of adultery is involved. This is unclean before Him. He promises judgment for those who commit adultery and fornication. Sometimes this judgment is physically enforced upon the person (babies, disease, etc) as they live. Here the body pays the price. But the soul will also receive spiritual judgment (to glory or damnation). Spiritually the act of adultery illustrates love of another god. Usually placing the self-god (what a person bows to) over the one true God. The act of adultery in a marriage represents the rejection of the husband's *headship* by the woman for another.

Ephesians 5:25-27 "Husbands, love your wives, even as Christ also loved the church, and gave himself for it; That he might sanctify and cleanse it with the washing of water by the word, That he might present it to himself a glorious church, not having spot, or wrinkle, or any such thing; but that it should be holy and without blemish."

Christ sanctifies and cleanses His children so he might present it to himself a glorious church, not having spot, or wrinkle, or any such thing; but that it should be holy and without blemish. We are talking about a spiritual cleanliness, not a literal physical cleanness. We are *washed* by the word of God. We must not forget that. His church is spiritually bound and under the authority of Christ. God's church being all of the wheat (or true believers) throughout time. In this manner the wives are also spiritually bound and under the spiritual authority of their husbands.

Ephesians 5:24 "Therefore as the church is subject unto Christ, so let the wives be to their own husbands in every thing."

But what if the wife has other ideas? She does not accept her *spiritual place* given to her by God. Or what if she desires to be the spiritual head of the household? This will result in rebellion to her husband as well as to God. Just as Adam and Eve were *caught naked* (and this is not referring to a sexual act) by disobeying the Word of God, so also is the wife here *spiritually* caught naked.

Jeremiah 3:8 "And I saw, when for all the causes whereby backsliding Israel committed adultery I had put her away, and given her a bill of divorce; yet her treacherous sister Judah feared not, but went and played the harlot also."

The act of adultery allows for divorce. Even for Almighty God. As we read in the Book of Jeremiah, God divorces Israel over its adultery. Please note in the Jeremiah verse who gives the bill of divorcement. It is God. And He gives this *bill authority* to the husband.

Deuteronomy 24:3-4 "And if the latter husband hate her, and write her a bill of divorcement, and giveth it in her hand, and sendeth her out of his house; or *if the latter husband die, which took her to be his wife; Her former husband, which sent her away, may not take her again to be his wife, after that she is <u>defiled</u>; for that is <u>abomination</u> before the LORD: and thou shalt not cause the <u>land</u> to sin, which the LORD thy God giveth thee for an inheritance."*

Hate #8130 a primitive root; to hate (personally)

Defiled #2930 a primitive root; to be foul, especially in a ceremonial or moral sense (contaminated)

Abomination #8441 prop. something disgusting (morally), i.e. (as noun) an abhorrence; especially idolatry or (concretely) an idol [feminine active participle of 8581 a primitive root; to loathe, i.e. (morally) detest]

Land #776 from an unused root probably meaning to be firm; the earth (at large, or partitively a land)

So you may ask, should we spiritualize this? Look at what this verse says. The marriage trail of a wife can cause the *land* to sin. (The actual land doesn't sin here, it is the people who do.) God is referring to us as *land*. If the wife remarries her husband (after another marriage in between) it is an abomination to Him. In other words, if a husband wants to remarry his ex-wife, it is okay. But if that ex-wife was married to someone else while she was away, that act caused her to be defiled. The woman is defiled. Why is this? Maybe the Book of Jeremiah can give us a clue.

Jeremiah 3:1 "They say, If a man put away his wife, and she go from him, and become another man's, shall he return unto her again? shall not that <u>land</u> be greatly <u>polluted</u>? but thou hast played the harlot with many lovers; yet return again to me, saith the LORD."

Land ##776 from an unused root probably meaning to be firm; the earth (at large, or partitively a land)

Polluted #2610 a primitive root; to soil, especially in a moral sense.

Harlot #2181 a primitive root [highly-fed and therefore wanton]; to commit adultery (usually of the female, and less often of simple fornication, rarely of involuntary ravishment); figuratively to commit idolatry (the Jewish people being regarded as the spouse of Jehovah)

Here we can clearly see the LORD referring to the woman as (#776) land. Advanced students may now apply this understanding of *land* to the Deuteronomy verse. God says that she is defiled and greatly polluted (morally foul and soiled) for her first husband. She is referred to as a harlot in the Jeremiah passage, and in Deuteronomy it is described as an abomination. God never uses these words lightly, therefore this subject matter of divorce and remarriage is very important. Let's look at the Matthew verse again.

Matthew 5:31-32 "It hath been said, Whosoever shall put away his wife, let him give her a writing of divorcement: But I say unto you, That whosoever shall put away his wife, saving for the cause of fornication, causeth her to commit adultery: and whosoever shall marry her that is divorced committeth adultery."

Divorcement #647 properly something separative, i.e. (specifically) divorce [neuter (gender) of a (presumed) adjective from a derivative of 868 to remove, i.e. (active) instigate to revolt; usually (reflexively) to desist, desert, etc.]

Fornication #4202 harlotry (including adultery and incest); fig. idolatry [from 4203 to act the harlot, i.e. (lit) indulge unlawful lust (of either sex) or (fig.) practice idolatry]

Adultery #3429 to commit adultery [from 3432 perhaps a primary word; a (male) paramour; fig. apostate]

In Matthew chapter 5, Jesus speaks to the multitude (the sermon on the mount), teaching them deeper understanding of what God's Will is for divorce and remarriage. Note that a man can "causeth her to commit adultery" by divorcing his wife outside of fornication.

Divorce in the Old Testament allows a wife to marry another. In the New Testament, the wife cannot marry again until ex-husband is dead. Why the difference? It is because the Holy Spirit will be poured out upon all flesh.

Matthew 19:8 "He saith unto them, Moses because of the hardness of your hearts suffered you to put away your wives: but from the beginning it was not so."

Hardness #4641 heard-heartedness, i.e. (specifically) <u>destitution of (spiritual) perception</u> [feminine of a compound of 4642 dry, i.e. hard or tough and 2588 the heart, i.e. (fig) the thoughts or feelings (mind)]

Hearts #4641 see above

Note that Jesus is telling them that it is because of their lack of *spiritual perception* (the hardness of their hearts) that the divorce was allowed. The pouring out of God's Spirit will change this spiritual perception in us. A marriage *loophole* is being closed.

Matthew 19:9 "And I say unto you, Whosoever shall put away his wife, except it be for fornication, and shall marry another, committeth adultery: and whoso marrieth her which is put away doth commit adultery."

Fornication #4202 **harlotry** (including adultery and incest); fig. **idolatry** [from 4203 to act the harlot, i.e. (lit) indulge unlawful lust or (fig) practice idolatry]

Many teach that this is not a Biblical reason for divorce today. Why? It's because God **hates** divorce. He does hate divorce, but Jesus says here "except it be for fornication". Case closed. So, other than fornication, any divorce is unlawful in God's sight. And these men can commit adultery just by marrying another woman. It seems like getting divorced has always been popular. This tells us that from the beginning, the institution of marriage was always a difficult situation to be in. It is a lifelong commitment. Just look at the reaction Jesus receives from His own disciples. His own Disciples!

Matthew 19:10 "His disciples say unto him, If the case of the man be so with his wife, it is not good to marry."

There are many observations one could make from this statement here. These male disciples wanted an out. They understood what Jesus was saying to them. Especially the spiritual responsibility placed upon them. They understood the limits God places on the *one flesh*. It makes them think if a marriage is profitable at all. And they do not want to place themselves in a position where they can cause others to commit adultery.

1 Corinthians 7:10-11 "And unto the married I command, yet not I, but the Lord, Let not the wife depart from her husband: But and if she depart, let her remain unmarried, or be reconciled to her husband: and let not the husband put away his wife."

Reconciled #2644 to change mutually, i.e. (fig.) to compound a difference [from 2596 a primary particle; (prepositional) down (in place or time) and 236 to make different]

Why does Paul teach that the wife should remain unmarried? Or that she should be "reconciled to her husband"? What difference does it make? Why is this important?

Romans 7:1-3 "Know ye not, brethren, (for I speak to them that know the law,) how that the law hath dominion over a man as long as he liveth? For the woman which hath an husband is bound by the law to her husband so long as he liveth; but if the husband be dead, she is loosed from the law of her husband. So then if, while her husband liveth, she be married to another man, she shall be called an adulteress: but if her husband be dead, she is free from that law; so that she is no adulteress, though she be married to another man."

The Law hath dominion over a man as long as he lives. The Law binds the woman who has a husband to him as long as he lives. If she marries another while her husband is still alive, she is to be called an adulteress. This teaches us that widows can remarry and not be called an adulteress. But it also teaches that an ex-wife still has a bond (because of the Law) with her ex-husband. What exactly is this *bond*?

1 Peter 3:7 "Likewise, ye husbands, dwell with them according to knowledge, giving honour unto the wife, as unto the weaker vessel, and as being heirs together of the grace of life; that your prayers be not hindered."

"Heirs together of the grace of life." As with the Ephesians verses discussed earlier (5:24-27), 1 Peter 3 teaches a spiritual connection between the one flesh. Note that these next verses reference spiritual relationships "unbelieving," "Holy," and "sanctified."

1 Corinthians 7:12-16 "But to the rest speak I, not the Lord: If any brother hath a wife that believeth not, and she be pleased to dwell with him, let him not put her away. And the woman which hath an husband that believeth not, and if he be pleased to dwell with her, let her not leave him. For the unbelieving husband is sanctified by the wife, and the unbelieving wife is sanctified by the husband: else were your children unclean; but now are they holy. But if the unbelieving depart, let him depart. A brother or a sister is not under bondage in such cases: but God hath called us to peace. For what knowest thou, O wife, whether thou shalt save thy husband? or how knowest thou, O man, whether thou shalt save thy wife?"

Sanctified #37 to make holy, i.e. (ceremonially) purify or consecrate (mentally) to venerate [from 40 (an awful thing) sacred]

Unclean #169 impure (ceremonially, morally [lewd] or specifically [demonic]) [from 1 the first (as a negative particle) and a presumed derivative of 2508 (meaning cleansed) to cleanse, i.e. (specifically) to prune; figurative to expiate]

Holy #40 from "hagos" (an awful thing) sacred (physically pure, morally blameless or religious, ceremonially consecrated [comp. 53 clean, i.e. (fig) innocent, modest, perfect]

Save #4982 from a primary "sos" (contraction for obsolete "saos" "safe"); to save i.e. deliver or protect (lit. or fig.)

Paul (with the Lord's Blessing) pleads for the mixed in belief couple to stay together. It is for the spouse (whether thou shalt save thy) and for the children. This is expressed for spiritual reasons, (not physical.) The focus is on salvation for the whole family. This is the marriage *mindset* God wants the Christian to have. Is this evident in most Christian unions? No. When you share the above Corinthians passages with people today, they ask "what does pleased to dwell" and "not under bondage" mean? In other words, do these verses allow me to leave my current terrible situation? Can I get a Divorce?

1 Corinthians 7:15 "But if the unbelieving depart, let him depart. A brother or a sister is not under bondage in such cases: but God hath called us to peace."

Pleased #4909 to think well of in common, i.e. assent to, feel gratified with [from 4862 a primary preposition denoting union; with or together and 2106 to think well of, approve]

Bondage #1402 to enslave (lit. or fig.) [from 1401 a slave (lit. or fig.. involuntary or voluntary; frequently, therefore in a qualified sense of subjection or subservience]

Peace #1515 probably from a primary verb "eiro" (to join); peace (lit. or fig.) by implication prosperity

"But God hath called us to peace." We are to be used of God *to join* others together with Him. That is, to be an instrument of joining together, not of tearing apart. Paul pleads to the Christian to serve the LORD here and not the self. This sacrifice is for the Glory of God.

People do not discern what is important here in these verses. Men and women have been placing their body's desires over their spiritual desires from very early on. This results in relationships of believe/believe not couples. Paul is telling us that the one spouse who believes brings the protection of God in to the household. Like in Exodus when the blood was put on the lintel and the two side posts of the doors of the Hebrews, the angel of death passed them by. This doesn't teach that unbelievers are eternally saved by the act of the spouse. No human being can save a person or sanctify anyone by their own power. But the believer does bring the presence of the Holy Spirit into a marriage relationship. Paul pleads with the reader to not take this away this opportunity from the unbeliever. They do not understand the big picture. We as Christians should understand this and make the sacrifice that is needed. There is no better way to serve our Lord Jesus Christ.

Hebrews 13:4 "Marriage is honourable in all, and the bed undefiled: but whoremongers and adulterers God will judge."

Marriage #1062 of uncertain affix; nuptials

Bed #2845 a couch; by extension cohabitation; by implication the male sperm [from 2749 to lie outstretched (literally or figuratively)]

Undefiled #283 unsoiled, i.e. (fig) pure [from 1 (as a neg. particle) the first & a derivative of 3392 to sully or taint, i.e. contaminate (ceremonially or morally)]

The marriage bed is a gift to us from God. He declares it to be "honourable in all" and "the bed undefiled." From His viewpoint, there is no judgment there. The husband is to love his wife and the wife is to submit to her husband. This is what Scripture teaches. This system works when we obey God's direction for our relationships. The problem is that we do not do it God's way. And because we do not obey His commands, there is a warning given to us from this verse in Hebrews. "Whoremongers and adulterers God will judge." We do not want to be judged by Him. Not like this. And this judgment from God does not mean that it awaits us after we die. This judgment can and is applied to us as we live and breathe. Remember King David and Bath-sheba? God settled the score during David's life. Spiritually, we reach our destination (heaven or hell) because we have made a decision long ago to head in that direction. God can and will help you achieve this goal. If you choose to commit adultery, you begin a chain reaction in your life. God reacts to your action. This will put you on a path away from Him. If you have chosen to commit adultery in your marriage, turn back now. You do not want to be judged of God on this. No relationship on earth is worth losing your eternal relationship with God in heaven.

In America, almost every person does not realize the importance of the marriage and how it relates to us spiritually.

Matthew 24:38 "For as in the days that were before the flood they were eating and drinking, marrying and giving in marriage, until the day that Noe entered into the ark, And knew not until the flood came, and took them all away; so shall also the coming of the Son of man be."

How many of these marriages in this Matthew passage do you think are pleasing to God? I suspect that many are re-marriages.

How can a woman who is "bound to her husband as long as he lives" marry another man? You ignore the Scripture verse completely or twist any truth away from it by combining human beliefs or understandings to it. Excuses like "God wouldn't want a person to go through that" or "that was for those people back then, not for us today", or whatever the human mind can come up with. Needless to say, there has been a lot of judgment applied by God to His creation over this issue. And many of the hearts of these people are now hardened. They will promote what they believe to others. Divorce is how we interpret it now. And the worst part of this is that there are now many Christians who believe that God allows these divorces and re-marriages. And they witness this opinion by their living example. They are actually leading others away from the very one who can keep their marriage together. We should look once again to the Scriptures and live according to the Word of God.

Proverb 5:18 "Let thy fountain be blessed: and rejoice with the wife of thy youth."

King Solomon

Much has been written about this man Solomon. Some teach that he is a depiction of Jesus Christ. I believe that Solomon is a spiritual representation of the Churches.

In Psalm 72, King David prays for his son Solomon. In this Psalm we see verses that describe a Spiritual rule or a headship. We read in the 13th verse of Psalm 72:

"He shall spare the poor and needy, and shall save the souls of the needy."

The throne of David is to be established before the LORD forever. (1 Kings 2:45) Here David is seen as a picture of the Lord Jesus Christ. (His throne is established forever.)

In 2 Chronicles, Solomon is offered this same arrangement from the LORD.

2 Chronicles 7:17-18 "And as for thee, if thou wilt walk before me, as David thy father walked, and do according to all that I have commanded thee, and shalt observe my statutes and my judgments; Then will I stablish the throne of thy kingdom, according as I have covenanted with David thy father, saying, There shall not fail thee a man to be ruler in Israel."

As the Throne is established for David (who Spiritually represents Christ), Solomon (who spiritually represents the *Church* or the Pastors and Priests who spread the Gospel) is given the same opportunity to establish his throne before the LORD. But he must *walk* as his father did. In addition, Solomon must live within the limits God decrees for a King.

Deuteronomy 17:16-17 "But he shall not multiply horses to himself, nor cause the people to return to Egypt, to the end that he should multiply horses: forasmuch as the LORD hath said unto you, Ye shall henceforth return no more that way. Neither shall he multiply wives to himself, that his heart turn not away: neither shall he greatly multiply to himself silver and gold."

There are two important spiritual commands from the LORD found here. First, He commands that a king is not to multiply horses nor cause the people to return to Egypt. "To the end that he should multiply horses:" Egypt is a destination and the people use horses to get there. What does the country of Egypt spiritually represent in this verse?

It is a place where the worship of false gods is prevalent, and of worshiping the LORD God in ways that do not please Him.

The horses are symbolic of Pastors, Priests, and the Prophets. They offer their different congregations many false belief systems. This is because very few of these spiritual leaders are from God. Most are from the seed of Satan that war with the Truth. They *cause* the people to return to Egypt (a place of spiritual bondage) by teaching them wrong doctrines. When King Solomon multiplies his horses (through his idolatry of false gods and their religions), he causes his people to fall away from worshiping the one true God. It is in this method that they spiritually *return* to Egypt.

The second important spiritual command from God is that a King is to not multiply wives to himself; neither shall he greatly multiply his silver and gold. This (multiply to himself) is referring to his personal earthly possessions. Gold, Silver and Wives are a possession. A wife (not multiple) is the limit. The LORD knows that one woman is plenty for a man. This way they can become the *one flesh*. Gold and silver is allowed to a King, he is just not to greatly multiply it. Why is this? It is because these earthly possessions will turn his heart away from God. This is a warning. And King Solomon did not heed it.

If we look at the essence of this man Solomon, we can see that as a picture of the Church he was destined to be overcome by those he was to oversee. His course of life spiritually represents the timeline of the church system from the start to the end. Both began their rule over the people with great promise and hope.

2 Chronicles 1:1 "And Solomon the son of David was strengthened in his kingdom, and the LORD his God was with him, and magnified him exceedingly."

Women seem to be very prevalent in the life of King Solomon. His mother Bathsheba (the wife of King David), the Queen of Sheba, and all his wives helped in directing his life and the choices he made. We know that in the end, Solomon's heart turns away from God. In chapter 2, we begin to see a pattern of submission to the females around him.

1 Kings 2:19 "Bathsheba therefore went unto king Solomon, to speak unto him for Adonijah. And the king rose up to meet her, and bowed himself unto her, and sat down on his throne, and caused a seat to be set for the king's mother; and she sat on his right hand."

Bowed #7812 to depress, i.e. prostrate (especially in homage to royalty or God)

Adonijah #138 lord (i.e. worshipper) of Jah.

Abishag #49 father of error (i.e. blundering)

When Solomon's mother approaches him, he does two very interesting things. One, he rises up and bows. This was a sign of submission to her. This word *bowed* stresses a heavy submission as opposed to lighter definitions that could have been used here. People suggest that Solomon was just honoring his mother, but they are missing important clues to what is spiritually taking place. Secondly, he caused a seat to be set up on his right hand for his mother. Here we can see that she possesses a tremendous influence over her son. Remember, Solomon has yet to receive 'Wisdom' from God. And so she sits in a position of authority. This honor was not given to her by God but from Solomon. The result is a challenge to the throne brought to him from within. Adonijah (the son of Haggith, a wife of David) asks Bath-sheba to request a marriage for him that would allow him to politically threaten her son's position as King. Bath-sheba without knowing (being deceived) brings this threat to him. She was asked this by Adonijah who wanted to marry Abishag, one of King David's concubine's. Solomon denies this request, and kills Adonijah. Bathsheba is not mentioned again. The *Church* (or Solomon) survives its first challenge of being compassed by others.

1 Kings 3:1-3 "And Solomon made affinity with Pharaoh king of Egypt, and took Pharaoh's daughter, and brought her into the city of David, until he had made an end of building his own house, and the house of the LORD, and the wall of Jerusalem round about. Only the people sacrificed in high places, because there was no house built unto the name of the LORD, until those days. And Solomon loved the LORD, walking in the statutes of David his father: only he sacrificed and burnt incense in high places."

Affinity #2859 to give (a daughter) away in marriage; to contract affinity by marriage

Solomon now begins his harem. Note that he marries an Egyptian and not a Hebrew woman. He brings this woman into the city of David until the house of the Lord is built. Now if Solomon represents the Church or the Spiritual leadership that builds the church, then the Egyptian woman represents the unsaved (tares) that enter in to this house of the LORD (as it is being built.) This should be a place to find God's Truth; therefore you must first know what this truth is. God comes to Solomon in a dream and tests him. "Ask what I shall give thee." (1 Kin 3:5) Solomon replies to this offer given him.

1 Kings 3:8-9 "And thy servant is in the midst of thy people which thou hast chosen, a great people, that cannot be numbered nor counted for multitude. Give therefore thy servant an understanding heart to judge thy people, that I may discern between good and bad: for who is able to judge this thy so great a people?"

A man of God needs wisdom to do what the LORD requires of him. The Church also needed this wisdom to do what God had designed it to do. This is not just a judicial wisdom, but spiritual

Wisdom. Judgments are made with God's Will in mind (first and foremost.) Leaders of the church are required to direct their congregation in this manner.

Note that the first test God brings to Solomon is to make a judgment between two harlots and a child. There are many interesting points in this judgment that provide us additional spiritual representations of the house of God. One woman (a harlot) calls Solomon lord twice and identifies herself as his handmaid. She is the one who tells us of what happened that night. The theft of the child happened at midnight, three days after she delivered. This was discovered in the daytime. This is the truth of the matter. She represents the wheat in this congregation. The other woman is trying to distort the truth. This (harlot) represents the tares in the congregation. The wheat here that would sacrifice all, in the end receives all. The tare here receives nothing. Her line is finished.

1 Kings 3:28 "And all Israel heard of the judgment which the king had judged; and they feared the king: for they saw that the wisdom of God was in him, to do judgment."

And so, the authority of the man of God (or Church) is established. But for how long?

In chapters 4 through 7, this authority of Solomon's *wisdom* builds God's Kingdom. This is in a literal sense as well as a spiritual sense. Note that Israel had 12 officers over all Israel to provide food (fruit) directly to the King. Even this structure of the (Political state) of Israel reflects the spiritual beginnings of God's Church system.

The Temple is built according to the explicit instructions given by God. A deeper study of the literal materials used, the literal measurements made, and all of the furnishings put within would illustrate to us additional spiritual representations of God's salvation plan. It was at this time that God's Wisdom flowed from Solomon like living water.

1 Kings 4:32-34 "And he spake three thousand proverbs: and his songs were a thousand and five. And he spake of trees, from the cedar tree that is in Lebanon even unto the hyssop that springeth out of the wall: he spake also of beasts, and of fowl, and of creeping things, and of fishes. And there came of all people to hear the wisdom of Solomon, from all kings of the earth, which had heard of his wisdom."

I find comparing the size of the house of the LORD to the house of Solomon interesting.

1 Kings 6:2-4 "And the house which king Solomon built for the LORD, the length thereof was threescore cubits, and the breadth thereof twenty cubits, and the height thereof thirty cubits. And the porch before the temple of the house, twenty cubits was the length thereof, according to the breadth of the house; and ten cubits was the breadth thereof before the house. And for the house he made windows of narrow lights."

The house was 90' x 30' x 45'. The porch was 30' x 15'. And windows of narrow lights.

1 Kings 7:2-5 "He built also the house of the forest of Lebanon; the length thereof was an hundred cubits, and the breadth thereof fifty cubits, and the height thereof thirty cubits, upon four rows of cedar pillars, with cedar beams upon the pillars. And it was covered with cedar above upon the beams, that lay on forty five pillars, fifteen in a row. And there were windows in three rows, and light was against light in three ranks. And all the doors and posts were square, with the windows: and light was against light in three ranks."

The house was 150' x 75' x 45'. The porch was 75' x 45'. And light was against light.

I do not understand why Solomon would build his house larger and more glorious than the house of the LORD, but interesting enough, the Churches of today (not all) reflect the wealth of the congregation. Some through they're many *windows*. I believe that Solomon was beginning to struggle in his walk with the LORD.

Notice how the Temple resembles a local congregation of today by just reading part of the prayer of Solomon as he dedicated this Temple to the LORD.

2 Chronicles 6:27 "Then hear thou from heaven, and forgive the sin of thy servants, and of thy people Israel, when thou hast taught them the good way, wherein they should walk; and send rain upon thy land, which thou hast given unto thy people for an inheritance."

In addition the Proverbs of Solomon sound like sermons from a Pastor or Priest. "My son, hear the instruction" "My son, forget not my law", "Hear me now therefore, O ye children", "My son, attend unto my wisdom, and bow thine ear to my understanding".

In 2 Chronicles 8, the Ark had been returned to the city of David. Solomon must now move his Egyptian wife out of the house of David. It is an issue of *Holiness.*

2 Chronicles 8:11 "And Solomon brought up the daughter of Pharaoh out of the city of David unto the house that he had built for her: for he said, My wife shall not dwell in the house of David king of Israel, because the places are holy, whereunto the ark of the LORD hath come."

In 1 Kings chapter 9, the LORD appears to Solomon (in a dream) and asks him again if he will walk before Him as his father David walked. Only this time, there is no response from Solomon recorded. This is a warning of the judgment that is to come from God.

A dispute of payment of cities due him from Hiram, the king of Tyre brings problems to Solomon's kingdom in the form of finances. He begins to force labor upon his people. And yet the Fame of Solomon grew and grew. Was this for Solomon or for his LORD?

Another woman now enters into Solomon's life. It is the Queen of Sheba.

1 Kings 10:1-3 "And when the queen of Sheba heard of the fame of Solomon concerning the name of the LORD, she came to prove him with hard questions. And she came to Jerusalem with a very great train, with camels that bare spices, and very much gold, and precious stones: and when she was come to Solomon, she communed with him of all that was in her heart. And Solomon told her all her questions:

there was not any thing hid from the king, which he told her not."

Prove #5254 a primitive root; to test, by implication to attempt

The Queen of Sheba came to prove King Solomon with hard questions. Actually, it is God who sends the test to him, using her to do so. Her criteria are using a woman's submission (she gathers information from him as a wife does from her husband), her (much gold) and the spices she brought to him. This relationship changes Solomon in very profound ways. He no longer feels restrained by limiting his gold or horses after their encounter. And when she leaves, Solomon disobeys God's commandments for a King completely. He spiritually declares war on the LORD through his actions in the land. What clues does the Bible give us regarding this change in Solomon and in the church that he spiritually represents?

1 Kings 10:4-5 "And when the queen of Sheba had seen all Solomon's wisdom, and the house that he had built, And the meat of his table, and the sitting of his servants, and the attendance of his ministers, and their apparel, and his cupbearers, and his ascent by which he went up unto the house of the LORD; there was no more spirit in her."

Spirit #7307 wind; by resemblance breath

In other words, He took her breath away by what she saw. She was entranced. She was trusting in the *man* representing God instead of trusting in the LORD. Note that she applies all of the possessions she sees to Solomon and not to God who gave them. She sees all of these physical manifestations as her proof and desires them.

1 Kings 10:6-9 "And she said to the king, It was a true report that I heard in mine own land of thy acts and of thy wisdom. Howbeit I believed not the words, until I came, and mine eyes had seen it: and, behold, the half was not told me: thy wisdom and prosperity exceedeth the fame which I heard. Happy are thy men, happy are these thy servants, which stand continually before thee, and that hear thy wisdom. Blessed be the LORD thy God, which delighted in thee, to set thee on the throne of Israel: because the LORD loved Israel for ever, therefore made he thee king, to do judgment and justice."

Six times in these verses she expresses *thy* (acts, wisdom, men, servants, etc.) She really pours it on if you examine these verses carefully. Teachers focus on, "Blessed be the LORD thy God" as proof that the Queen of Sheba became saved, but don't miss that the focus is really on all of Solomon's possessions and on his personal wisdom. People in the congregation do this all of the time. They place their trust (and subsequently their works) in their Pastor or Priest. The relationship is with the representative and not with God Himself. This is part of the test Solomon receives from God. His pride is tested and he fails.

1 Kings 10:10 "And she gave the king an hundred and twenty talents of gold, and of spices very great store, and precious stones: there came no more such abundance of spices as these which the queen of Sheba gave to king Solomon."

The actual number one hundred and twenty is used 6 times in Scripture. It usage is very interesting. God sets limits on mankind of 120 years. (Genesis 6) The sons of Kohath: Uriel the chief and his brethren number 120. (1 Chronicles 15) The 120 is the amount of gold the Queen of Sheba gives to Solomon. (1 Kings 10 & 2 Chronicles 9) The 120 princes Darius sets up over his kingdom. (Daniel 6) And Peter the Apostle stands up in the midst of the disciples-the number of names were about 120. (Acts 1) In each case, the number 120 identifies with a limit from God for a special purpose. It becomes a sign to the World. The 120 years (time), the sons of Kohath (they are in charge of a special section of the Tabernacle), the 120 princes (to rule over the land), about 120 (names together) with Peter (a spiritual group). In this 1 Kings verse God is giving us a set number of gold talents as a sign (the future fall of Solomon that is to come.) But the main focus here is on the spices. God makes note of the amount of spices given to Solomon.

Spices #1314 fragrance; by implication spicery; also the balsam plant [from the same as 1313 to be fragrant]

We Christians have a certain odor. Our *works* produces a *sweat* that God can smell.

Philippians 4:18 "But I have all, and abound: I am full, having received of Epaphroditus the things which were sent from you, an odour of a sweet smell, a sacrifice acceptable, wellpleasing to God."

Solomon was overwhelmed by the amount of spices (and the odor of it.) I believe that this is a spiritual picture of Solomon (as the Church) being overwhelmed by the smell or works of the congregation (Queen of Sheba.) What God *smelled* in Solomon was not the odor He wanted to smell from him. His sacrifice was not well pleasing to the LORD.

We read in the book of Jeremiah, this is not the only time God smells something wrong.

Jeremiah 6:20 "To what purpose cometh there to me incense from Sheba, and the sweet cane from a far country? your burnt offerings are not acceptable, nor your sacrifices sweet unto me."

References to smells abound in the Song of Solomon (as does descriptions of body parts.) Solomon's relationship to his LORD is described as having been *one flesh* with Him. But separation keeps occurring and forces him to look for his beloved. Twice, *watchmen* find and correct him. Does this represent God's two visits to him in dreams? Note that Lebanon is used in various ways describing his relationship to God but not Jerusalem.

Song of Solomon 8:11-12 "Solomon had a vineyard at Baalhamon; he let out the vineyard unto keepers; every one for the fruit thereof was to bring a thousand pieces of silver. My vineyard, which is mine, is before me: thou, O Solomon, must have a thousand, and those that keep the fruit thereof two hundred."

The 120 shows up again (1,200) displaying to us another limit in a Solomon's vineyard.

2 Chronicles 9:10-11 "And the servants also of Huram, and the servants of Solomon, which brought gold from Ophir, brought algum trees and precious stones. And the king made of the algum trees terraces to the house of the LORD, and to the king's palace, and harps and psalteries for singers: and there were none such seen before in the land of Judah."

We read in 2 Kings 10 that a great plenty of Algum trees are brought unto Solomon. "There came no such almug trees, nor were seen unto this day." He produces harps and psalteries from them. The language of 'None such seen before' appears to me that they are calling attention to themselves. The other use of the trees however, makes me question where the heart of Solomon is directed. Is it to himself or to the LORD?

2 Chronicles 5:1 "Thus all the work that Solomon made for the house of the LORD was finished: and Solomon brought in all the things that David his father had dedicated; and the silver, and the gold, and all the instruments, put he among the treasures of the house of God."

All the work was finished. Gold, instruments, and other items dedicated by David were put in the house of God. But Solomon wanted to add to this. He takes these almug trees and makes *steps* to enter the House of the LORD. I do not believe that God approved this addition. This was not in the original blueprint. King Solomon was picked to build the house of God; the problem was that he didn't know when to stop. Please note that the Church also added on to its original *blueprint* throughout the years.

2 Chronicles 9:12 "And king Solomon gave to the queen of Sheba all her desire, whatsoever she asked, beside that which she had brought unto the king. So she turned, and went away to her own land, she and her servants."

The test of Solomon (representing the Church) from Sheba is over. He gave to her all that she desired, whatsoever she asked. This was not a good move. Churches are not to give to their congregations everything they want. This displays another example of Solomon's submission to the women in his life. (Spiritually this represents the Church submitting to the wants of its members.) And we can tie this in with another Judge of God who gave to his woman all that she desired. That woman's name was Delilah. She vexed Samson until he gave in to her. His *rule* over the people quickly came to an end.

2 Chronicles 9:13 "Now the weight of gold that came to Solomon in one year was six hundred and threescore and six talents of gold;"

Six hundred and threescore and six talents of gold = 666. Now where have I heard of this number before?

Revelation 13:18 "Here is wisdom. Let him that hath understanding count the number of the beast: for it is the number of a man; and his number is Six hundred threescore and six."

Is this *man* Solomon (by what he spiritually represents)? Many believe that this man is Satan. Others believe it to be an actual person (now alive or still to come.) What is man?

Man #444 Man-faced, i.e. a human being [from 435 a man & (the countenance from 3700 to gaze, i.e. with wide opened eyes)]

Note, that this is not describing #435, which is just a man (properly as an individual male.) It is Man-faced (#444). The number 666 also identifies with Satan and his earthly kingdom.

Here in Revelation this number 666 identifies with men with wide opened eyes, or men who are given the truth of God. Those who carry spiritual responsibility to others.

King Solomon is identified with the number 666 in these Old Testament verses. He was given the truth of God and the responsibility to shepherd others with this knowledge.

I believe God makes a spiritual judgment on Solomon. Right after the Queen of Sheba leaves to her own country, God *blesses* Solomon with this weight in gold. (666 talents)

1 Kings 10:14 "Now the weight of gold that came to Solomon in one year was six hundred threescore and six talents of gold,"

The Queen of Sheba proved him all right! After this *blessing* of gold, Solomon falls away from the truth quickly.

2 Chronicles 9:14 "Beside that which chapmen and merchants brought. And all the kings of Arabia and governors of the country brought gold and silver to Solomon."

Gold begins to pour into Solomon's Kingdom. And he begins to get creative with what he does with it. Solomon now (adds on) to his Temple house.

Targets #6793 a hook (as pointed); also a large shield (as if guarding by prickliness) [from feminine of 6791 to be prickly; a thorn]

Shields #4043 shield (small one or buckler); fig. a protector; also the scaly hide of the crocodile [from feminine of 1598 to hedge about, i.e. protect]

2 Chronicles 9:15-20 "And king Solomon made two hundred targets of beaten gold: six hundred shekels of beaten gold went to one target. And three hundred shields made he of beaten gold: three hundred shekels of gold went to one shield. And the king put them in the house of the forest of Lebanon. Moreover the king made a great throne of ivory, and overlaid it with pure gold. And there were six steps to the throne, with a footstool of gold, which were fastened to the throne, and stays on each side of the sitting place, and two lions standing by the stays: And twelve lions stood there on the one side and on the other upon the six steps. There was not the like made in any kingdom. And all the drinking vessels of king Solomon were of gold, and all the vessels of the house of the forest of Lebanon were of pure gold: none were of silver; it was not any thing accounted of in the days of Solomon."

To me, this is a description of the Temple of God on earth. Man's version of course. Solomon continues to enhance this house with his *multiplied* Gold. Soon he will build temples to other *gods.* He makes an ivory throne for himself and covers it with pure gold. Is this a representation of the throne of Satan? We know that Satan goes about as a roaring lion seeking those he can devour, using his seed (false representations of God) to war against the Truth. These men have a position of spiritual authority. Does the abomination of desolation sit in this ivory throne? God will deal with thrones of ivory.

Amos 3:15 "And I will smite the winter house with the summer house; and the houses of ivory shall perish, and the great houses shall have an end, saith the LORD."

Someone who admits they have not the understanding of a *man*, and did not learn wisdom or have the knowledge of the holy, shares a indispensable lesson in Proverbs.

Proverb 30:5 "Every word of God is pure: he is a shield unto them that put their trust in him."

Every word of God is pure. God taught Solomon serious guidelines that he needed to follow. The most important was that he was to put his trust in the LORD. The same as those who were chosen to lead the church. But Solomon did not *walk* as his father David did before the LORD. And so he begins to break every commandment he was given by God.

Deuteronomy 17:16-17 "But he shall not multiply horses to himself, nor cause the people to return to Egypt, to the end that he should multiply horses: forasmuch as the LORD hath said unto you, Ye shall henceforth return no more that way. Neither shall he multiply wives to himself, that his heart turn not away: neither shall he greatly multiply to himself silver and gold."

King Solomon greatly multiplied to himself gold.

2 Chronicles 9:22 "And king Solomon passed all the kings of the earth in riches and wisdom."

He multiplied horses to himself.

2 Chronicles 9:25 "And Solomon had four thousand stalls for horses and chariots, and twelve thousand horsemen; whom he bestowed in the chariot cities, and with the king at Jerusalem."

He involved Egypt with his horses.

2 Chronicles 9:28 "And they brought unto Solomon horses out of Egypt, and out of all lands."

Now that God has passed a Judgment on Solomon, it seems that his restraint to sin is completely gone. He is ready for the third woman in his life. Many "strange women".

1 Kings 11:1-3 "But king Solomon loved many strange women, together with the daughter of Pharaoh, women of the Moabites, Ammonites, Edomites, Zidonians, and Hittites; Of the nations concerning which the LORD said unto the children of Israel, Ye shall not go in to them, neither shall they come in unto you: for surely they will turn away your heart after their gods: Solomon clave unto these in love. And he had seven hundred wives, princesses, and three hundred concubines: and his wives turned away his heart."

Solomon knew that these actions were forbidden. God even told him what the result would be. Note that his wife, (the daughter of Pharaoh) is also listed as a strange woman.

Solomon multiplies his wives. Why would he do this? He didn't need to. He didn't have to marry daughters of his rivals for safety. He could trust in God to protect Israel. But that's not why he did this. We read "Solomon clave unto these in love." He loved these women more than He loved his God. The result was that his heart turned away from God. Now, you might ask, how can this relate to a Church? The Church of today does not teach or lead strictly according to Scripture. Throughout time, the Church authority has twisted the teaching and understanding of God's Word so much that what we are taught now is very superficial. The spiritual roles of men and women today are far away from what they were created to be. Women are to be silent in the church. For many reasons, the church does not teach this because it no longer knows how to do so. There are so many variations of *truth* now; that the real Truth is hidden. Solomon's wives and the princesses spiritually represent these variations. The concubines (the unmarried wives) bring in even more strange additions to this.

1 Kings 11:4 "For it came to pass, when Solomon was old, that his wives turned away his heart after other gods: and his heart was not perfect with the LORD his God, as was the heart of David his father."

This turning away from God took time. At the end of his reign, Solomon had long forgotten how to worship correctly. And God compares his heart to the heart of his father David here. The Bible shows us two of Solomon's favorites, Ashtoreth and Milcom.

Ashtoreth #6252 the name of a Sidonian deity [plural of 6251 increase]

Zidonians #6722 a Tsidonian [partial from 6721 fishery (in the sense of catching fish)]

Milcom #4445 Malcam, national idol [from 4428 king for 4432 Molek]

Ammonites #5984 an Ammonite [patronymic from 5983 tribal, i.e. inbred]

1 Kings 11:5-6 "For Solomon went after Ashtoreth the goddess of the Zidonians, and after Milcom the abomination of the Ammonites. And Solomon did evil in the sight of the LORD, and went not fully after the LORD, as did David his father."

My guess is that he preferred their *worship service* to JEHOVAH's. This is evil in the sight of the LORD. Note that he "went not fully after the LORD." People do this all the time. They want to worship other idols in their life. But to someone who is to bring the Gospel to the World this is devastating. Especially to someone who *knows* the Truth.

1 Kings 11:7-8 "Then did Solomon build an high place for Chemosh, the abomination of Moab, in the hill that is before Jerusalem, and for Molech, the abomination of the children of Ammon. And likewise did he for all his strange wives, which burnt incense and sacrificed unto their gods."

Another 'god' Solomon worships is named Chemosh. He builds his high place.

Chemosh #3645 to subdue; the powerful; Kemosh, the god of the Moabites

Moab # 4124 Moab; from (her [the mother's]) father; an incestuous son of Lot]

The worst thing that someone in a spiritual position of authority can do is to lead his people astray. Isn't this what the antichrist is suppose to do? Two of these *gods* are related to Israel through Lot. His incest with his two daughters brought about the races of the Ammonites and the Moabites. Note that each time this act was committed the two daughters gave their father wine to make him unaware of what was happening. The seed that the daughters wanted preserved have their own gods. And now Solomon (who is a representation of the men of God) is now worshipping them. The third god is the female deity Ashtoreth. Solomon shows us that his submission to women is complete. He is now worthless to bring the Gospel to the World because he has become just like the World. All of the religions become one. Question: what incense were they using?

2 Kings 23:13 "And the high places that were before Jerusalem, which were on the right hand of the mount of corruption, which Solomon the king of Israel had builded for Ashtoreth the abomination of the Zidonians, and for Chemosh the abomination of the Moabites, and for Milcom the abomination of the children of Ammon, did the king defile."

Solomon likes to put things on the right hand. His Mother Bathsheba was given a seat of authority (on his right), and now Solomon builds high places on the right hand of the mount of corruption. In Hebrews 1:3, Jesus Christ sits down on the right hand of the Majesty on high. Solomon really misses the mark on this. His heart was turned away.

1 Kings 11:9-10 "And the LORD was angry with Solomon, because his heart was turned from the LORD God of Israel, which had appeared unto him twice, And had commanded him concerning this thing, that he should not go after other gods: but he kept not that which the LORD commanded."

The church, which has the authority of God, must do what God commands. The LORD appeared to Solomon twice. He witnesses to him two times. That's all Solomon gets.

1 Kings 11:11-13 "Wherefore the LORD said unto Solomon, Forasmuch as this is done of thee, and thou hast not kept my covenant and my statutes, which I have commanded thee, I will surely rend the kingdom from thee, and will give it to thy servant. Notwithstanding in thy days I will not do it for David thy father's sake: but I will rend it out of the hand of thy son. Howbeit I will not rend away all the kingdom; but will give one tribe to thy son for David my servant's sake, and for Jerusalem's sake which I have chosen."

When the sons of God saw that the daughters of men were fair (Genesis 6:1), they took them wives of all which they chose. (Solomon also did this.) In Genesis, God decreed a limit of 120 years for mankind. He gives Solomon a similar sign by recording the 120 talents of Gold given to him. In Genesis the unions produced offspring (giants). These Giants who became mighty men of renown replaced the sons of God. These *giants* would lead the human race away from God. This was the case with Solomon. The LORD had to make an end of the direction he was taking Israel. This study of Solomon shows us a complete failure of someone who was to represent God on earth. This spiritual picture of authority being overcome is repeated over and over in Scripture. The influence of women on men of God is illustrated both here and in Genesis. What has started in the Garden of Eden (the Spiritual relationship between men and women) continues here.

Pentecost

Luke 23:28-29 "But Jesus turning unto them said, Daughters of Jerusalem, weep not for me, but weep for yourselves, and for your children. For, behold, the days are coming, in the which they shall say, Blessed are the barren, and the wombs that never bare, and the paps which never gave suck."

As Jesus Christ is being led away to His crucifixion, He turns to the great company of women who were crying and lamenting for Him. (Simon the Cyrenian carrying His cross at this time.) A beaten and bloody Jesus tells these women to "weep for yourselves and for your children." He goes on to explain that the days will come when they shall say *blessed* are the barren. What does Jesus mean by this statement?

Blessed #3107 Supremely blest; by extension fortunate well off

This word is used many times in the *Beatitudes*, also known as the Sermon on the Mount found in Matthew chapter 5. Jesus is telling this company of women that there will come a time when "they shall say." Notice that in the next verse we read, "then shall they begin to say to the mountains, fall on us; and to the hills, cover us."

This shows us a time reference, when this proclamation is to take place.

Luke 23:30 "Then shall they begin to say to the mountains, Fall on us; and to the hills, Cover us."

The days are coming in which they shall say, "Blessed are the barren, and the wombs that never bare, and the paps which never gave suck." Women would be used as a *sign* in the sense that their natural function of childbirth is viewed more as a curse than as a blessing from God. THEN, shall they begin to say to the mountains "fall on us." When one asks for a mountain to fall on them, it is generally understood that they want something to be between them and God. So they may be hidden from view. This is a true conclusion. But when does this request for a mountain covering actually begin? Is it at the Day of Judgment, as many believe? These verses in Luke clearly give us clues as to when this *time* begins. That time is very close. Jesus states "the days are coming" and yet He tells the women present to weep for yourselves and for your children. What is going on? Does Jesus really mean what He says to these women and their children? The common understanding of these passages is that 'those days' (sometime in the far future) it will be so physically terrible for mankind that it would be better if one did not have a child around to experience it. But what if 'those days' actually began at Pentecost? What if the act of God's Spirit being poured out upon all flesh marked the beginning of 'those days'? Please note that the focus here is not primarily on the children, but on the female gender as a whole. Once again the woman is referenced as a sign to the world. I believe that those days cover the time period from Pentecost to the Day of Judgment. We read in the next verse of Luke.

Luke 23:31 "For if they do these things in a green tree, what shall be done in the dry?"

This verse describes two time periods. One period that begins at Pentecost (a green tree), and one period for the Final Tribulation (dry). The green tree is watered and cared for (the period of the Holy Spirit being poured out). It brings forth *fruit* from the field.

Psalms 104:30 "Thou sendest forth thy spirit, they are created: and thou renewest the face of the earth (#127)."

Note that God uses #127 Earth here. This pouring out of God's Spirit brings spiritual growth to those who receive this. What a Blessed time. Good fruit that is brought forth and the face of the earth are renewed. These daughters of Jerusalem that Jesus speaks to will live during this *green tree* time period. But then comes the dry. The dry receives no water (God's Spirit) from above.

We read in the Book of Joel the prophesy of this green tree time period.

Joel 2:28-29 "And it shall come to pass afterward, that I will pour out my spirit upon all flesh; and your sons and your daughters shall prophesy, your old men shall dream dreams, your young men shall see visions: And also upon the servants and upon the handmaids in those days will I pour out my spirit."

These verses are perhaps is the most notable in the entire Book of Joel. It is a prophesy of the Holy Spirit being poured out upon all flesh. This pouring out of the Spirit changed mankind's spiritual relationship to God. Teachers today do not comprehend the different relationships that were formed by this action. They tend to believe that the spiritual reactions to this pouring out (prophesy, dreams, and visions) are really the same response. Their conclusion of this passage ignores the spiritual headship given here by God. This prophecy of Joel's was fulfilled at Pentecost when God's servants & handmaids received this pouring out of God's Spirit, and, as we read in Acts was also poured upon all flesh.

Acts 2:16-18 "But this is that which was spoken by the prophet Joel; And it shall come to pass in the last days, saith God, I will pour out of my Spirit upon all flesh: and your sons and your daughters shall prophesy, and your young men shall see visions, and your old men shall dream dreams: And on my servants and on my handmaidens I will pour out in those days of my Spirit; and they shall prophesy:"

As we read in both the Joel and Acts passages, we see a *your* and *my* designation. God will direct His Spirit toward two classes. Toward my people and your people. But before we explain who these two classes of people are, we need to take an overall view of the Book of Joel.

Joel 1:1 "The word of the LORD that came to Joel the son of Pethuel."

Joel #3100 Jehovah (is his) God
Pethuel #6602 Enlarged of God

Joel is well qualified to say the things he is about to say. He is a true prophet of the LORD. Overall, the Book of Joel gives us a view of God's Spirit in the life of His Creation (Mankind). In Chapter one, we read about the Priests of the Old Testament and how the Word (Truth) becomes cut off from them. In chapter two, we read the day of the LORD cometh, for it is nigh at hand. It is always the darkest before the dawn. Joel describes this darkness (a complete lack of Truth) in the Spiritual leaders of that day. God allowed this to happen in order to prepare mankind for the coming of the Messiah. He tells mankind during this time to cry out to Him. In verses 18 to 27, God hears His people and sends Jesus Christ to mankind. This restores the corn, and wine, and oil. And the years lost by what the locust, etc… has eaten. In verse 28, God pours out His Spirit (Pentecost), and the Church system begins. Chapter 3 tells us of the Great Tribulation period and the Judgment that comes from God. The book ends with a description of life after the Judgment. Now back to the two classes of people.

Joel 2:28-29 "And it shall come to pass afterward, that I will pour out my spirit upon all flesh; and your sons and your daughters shall prophesy, your old men shall dream dreams, your young men shall see visions: And also upon the servants and upon the handmaids in those days will I pour out my spirit."

To fully understand what is being taught in these verses, we must know the definitions of the words used. First we look at the Old Testament words used in the Book of Joel.

Pour #8210 primitive root; to spill forth (blood, a libation, liquid metal; or even a solid, i.e. to mound up); (fig.) to expend (life, soul, complaint, money); intens. to sprawl out.

Spirit #7307 wind; by resemblance breath, i.e. a sensible (or even violent) exhalation; fig. life, anger, unsubstantiality; by extension a region of the sky; by resemblance spirit, but only of a rational being (including its expression and functions) [from 7306 a primitive root; properly to blow, i.e. breathe; only (literal) to smell or (by implication) perceive (figuratively to anticipate, enjoy)]

All #3605 properly the whole; hence, all, any or every (in the singular only, but often in a plural sense) [from 3634 a primitive root; to complete]

Flesh #1320 Flesh (from its freshness); by extension body, person; also (by euphemism) the pudenda of a man [from 1319 to be fresh, i.e. full (rosy, (fig) cheerful); to announce]

Prophesy #5012 a primitive root; to prophesy, i.e. speak (or sing) by inspiration (in prediction or simple discourse)

Dream #2492 a primitive root; properly to bind firmly, i.e. (by implication) to be (causative to make) plump; also (through the figurative sense of dumbness) to dream

Dreams #2472 a dream [from 2492]

Visions #2384 a revelation, especially by dream [from 2372 a primitive root; to gaze at; mentally To perceive, contemplate (with pleasure); specifically to have a vision of]

Now we review the New Testament definitions of the same words in the Book of Acts.

Pour #1632 to pour forth; (fig.) to bestow [from 1537 origin, from; (fig) direct or remote]

My (Spirit of Me) #3450 of me, the simpler form of [1700 a prol. form of 3450; of me]

Spirit #4151 a current of air, i.e. breath (blast) or a breeze; by analogy or figuratively a spirit, i.e. (human) the rational soul, (by implication) vital principle, mental disposition, etc., or (superhuman) an angel, demon, or (divine) God, Christ's spirit, the Holy Spirit [from 4154 a primary word; to breathe hard, i.e. breeze]

On #1909 a primary preposition; properly meaning superimposition (of time, place, order, etc.) as a relation of distribution [with the gen.] i.e. over, upon, etc.; of rest (with the dative) at, on, etc.; of direction (with the accusative) toward, upon, etc.

All #3956 including all the forms of declension; apparently a primary word; all, any, every, the whole.

Flesh #4561 flesh (as stripped of the skin), i.e. (strictly) the meat of an animal (as food), or (by extension) the body (as opposed to the soul [or spirit], or as the symbol of what is external, or as the means of kindred), or (by implication) human nature (with its frailties and passions), or (spec.) a human being (as such) [prob. from the base of 4563 broom]

Prophesy #4395 to foretell events, divine, speak under inspiration, exercise the prophetic office [from 4396 a foreteller ("prophet"); by anal. an inspired speaker, by extens. a poet]

Visions #3706 the act of gazing, i.e. (external) an aspect or (internally) an inspired appearance [from 3708 properly to stare at, i.e. (by implication) to discern clearly (phys. or mentally); by extension to attend to; by Hebraism To experience; passively to appear]

Dream #1798 something seen in sleep, i.e. a dream (vision in a dream) [from 1722 a primary preposition denoting (fixed) position (in time, place, or state), & (by implication) instrumentality (medially or constructively), i.e. a relation of rest; "in", at, (up-) on, by and 5258 sleep, i.e. (fig) spiritual torpor]

Dreams #1797 to dream [from 1798]

This is a spiritual communication. All through the Bible, God *connects* with a human being through a dream, a vision, or His Word comes upon them. Shortly afterward an emotional physical response (fear, anger, confidence, obstinacy) from that person ensues. God directs the path of that person in this manner. These dreams and visions will happen to (your) old and young men when God's Spirit is poured out to all flesh. The men of Job completely understood what these dreams and visions meant to them.

Job 4:12-14 "Now a thing was secretly brought to me, and mine ear received a little thereof. In thoughts from the visions of the night, when deep sleep falleth on men, Fear came upon me, and trembling, which made all my bones to shake."

Job 7:13-14 "When I say, My bed shall comfort me, my couch shall ease my complaint; Then thou scarest me with dreams, and terrifiest me through visions:"

Job 33:12-18 "Behold, in this thou art not just: I will answer thee, that God is greater than man. Why dost thou strive against him? for he giveth not account of any of his matters. For God speaketh once, yea twice, yet man perceiveth it not. In a dream, in a vision of the night, when deep sleep falleth upon men, in slumberings upon the bed; Then he openeth the ears of men, and sealeth their instruction, That he may withdraw man from his purpose, and hide pride from man. He keepeth back his soul from the pit, and his life from perishing by the sword."

Proverb 29:17-18 "Correct thy son, and he shall give thee rest; yea, he shall give delight unto thy soul. Where there is no vision, the people perish: but he that keepeth the law, happy is he."

God will direct the old and young men in this way (from Pentecost on). In order for the husband to be the spiritual leader of his family, and in order to give an account to God in how he performed this task, the man needs direct instructions from the Holy Spirit.

Matthew 24:45-46 "Who then is a faithful and wise servant, whom his lord hath made ruler over his household, to give them meat in due season? Blessed is that servant, whom his lord when he cometh shall find so doing."

When the Holy Spirit is poured out, God spiritually leads each man. To dream or to see a vision is to have God send a message to you. This will direct your *desires*. And this method of spiritual communication begins at Pentecost and lasts to the Great Tribulation. With this information we can now look at *your* and *my* class of people.

Acts 2:5 "And there were dwelling at Jerusalem Jews, devout men, out of every nation under heaven."

Peter addresses the crowd that is gathered around the place where this special event just occurred. This was spoken to the men who had arrived there for the feast of Pentecost.

Acts 2:14 "But Peter, standing up with the eleven, lifted up his voice, and said unto them, Ye men of Judaea, and all ye that dwell at Jerusalem, be this known unto you, and hearken to my words:"

Peter is addressing Jews and men of Judaea in this crowd. He is referring to them as 'your'. They are the same nationality as Peter, but he refers to them as your. These Jews will represent those out in the world that will receive this pouring out of the Spirit.

Acts 2:8 "And how hear we every man in our own tongue, wherein we were born? Parthians, and Medes, and Elamites, and the dwellers in Mesopotamia, and in Judaea, and Cappadocia, in Pontus, and Asia, Phrygia, and Pamphylia, in Egypt, and in the parts of Libya about Cyrene, and strangers of Rome, Jews and proselytes, Cretes and Arabians, we do hear them speak in our tongues the wonderful works of God."

These men spiritually represent the Gentiles of the world that now have an opportunity to receive Salvation from God Almighty. This is the *your* classification.

Acts 2:17 "And it shall come to pass in the last days, saith God, I will pour out of my Spirit upon all flesh: and your sons and your daughters shall prophesy, and your young men shall see visions, and your old men shall dream dreams:"

The Spirit of God will be poured out upon all Gentile flesh and spiritual reactions (prophesy, visions and dreams) began to manifest within them. An example of daughters that prophesy is found in Acts chapter 21.

Acts 21:8-9 "And the next day we that were of Paul's company departed, and came unto Caesarea: and we entered into the house of Philip the evangelist, which was one of the seven; and abode with him. And the same man had four daughters, virgins, which did prophesy."

Please note that these four daughters are virgins; they have never known a man. They are still under their father's authority (or spiritual covering) in the home.

Acts 2:18 "And on my servants and on my handmaidens I will pour out in those days of my Spirit; and they shall prophesy:"

Servants #1401 a slave (lit or fig, involuntary or voluntary; frequently, therefore in a qualified sense of subjection or subserviency) [from 1210 a primary verb; to bind (in various applications, literally or figuratively]

Handmaidens #1399 feminine of 1401; a female slave (involuntary or voluntary)

Peter is one of these servants. He is a slave to God. He is (bound) by the Holy Spirit.

He will prophesy. He will speak under inspiration and exercise the prophetic office. Mary (The human mother of Jesus) is an example of a New Testament handmaid.

Luke 1:38 "And Mary said, Behold the handmaid of the Lord; be it unto me according to thy word. And the angel departed from her."

Please note that in these Joel/Acts verses, it is not just the immediate son or daughter that is being addressed here. God's servants and handmaids transcend generations of mankind, as does these sons and daughters. This is the *my* classification. But how does this pouring out of God's Spirit upon all flesh fit in with the Luke verses? There is an interesting point not to be missed here. Look at the Acts 2:17 verse again.

Acts 2:17 "And it shall come to pass in the last days, saith God, I will pour out of my Spirit upon all flesh: and your sons and your daughters shall prophesy, and your young men shall see visions, and your old men shall dream dreams:"

Don't miss the time reference here. We are in the last days. So, who is missing here? What family member is not mentioned? It is the woman or the wife. Your *women* are not mentioned in the Joel or Acts verses. We just read about sons and daughters, and young and old men. Why is this? Why is the woman or wife left out here?

Ephesians 5:31-32 "For this cause shall a man leave his father and mother, and shall be joined unto his wife, and they two shall be one flesh. This is a great mystery: but I speak concerning Christ and the church."

Is the reason because when a man and woman get married, they become 'one flesh'? No need to list them separately? Or it is that back then the culture was so repressive upon women; the writer didn't include them (for that very reason)? Is this true? First of all, I have never believed that the culture of the day altered the message God decreed for His Word. We are to follow all the spiritual guidelines set forth in Scripture just as they had to follow them back in the day. We cannot push these spiritual guidelines away by simply stating, "Because the physical sacrifices of the Old Testament are gone, so then is all of the spiritual teachings that were attached to them." Our problem today is that almost all of the current Pastors, Priests or teachers do not grasp these important spiritual guidelines from the Bible. The spiritual discernment of this (over many generations) has become so integrated with the ideas of mankind that the real truth is hidden from us. And this understanding has been taught to the next generation and so on. But we know the Bible teaches us that what God has taught from the beginning is still to be taught today.

Psalm 33:11 "The counsel of the LORD standeth for ever, the thoughts of his heart to all generations."

This verse in Psalms is not just for basic Biblical teachings. It also teaches that the deep things of God "standeth for ever." So the culture of the day or the times that we live in do not alter any of the core doctrines taught in Scripture. So we come back to our original question. Why is the woman or wife not mentioned in these last day verses?

1 Corinthians 11:3-7 "But I would have you know, that the head of every man is Christ; and the head of the woman is the man; and the head of Christ is God. Every man praying or prophesying, having his head covered, dishonoureth his head. But every woman that prayeth or prophesieth with her head uncovered dishonoureth her head: for that is even all one as if she were shaven. For if the woman be not covered, let her also be shorn: but if it be a shame for a woman to be shorn or shaven, let her be covered. For a man indeed ought not to cover

his head, forasmuch as he is the image and glory of God: but the woman is the glory of the man."

These verses in 1 Corinthians give us a huge clue. They teach spiritual authority. The man is the head of the woman. This is a spiritual headship. In order for the man to lead his household, God uses the Holy Spirit to help the man in this. If the Holy Spirit taught both the man and the woman the same, then there would be no need for a spiritual *head* in the home. We remember in Numbers the lesson of Aaron and Miriam the Prophetess.

Numbers 12:6 "And he said, Hear now my words: If there be a prophet among you, I the LORD will make myself known unto him in a vision, and will speak unto him in a dream."

This has been consistent for men in the Scriptures. We read about Joseph, the husband of Mary. He receives 3 dreams from the angel of the Lord. (Matt 1:20, 2:13, and 2:19) In addition the wise men that sought Jesus also received a dream. (Matt 2:12) And now at Pentecost, all of the old and the young men are now included. In both of these Joel and Acts passages, we see a spiritual authority for each and every person listed there. God Himself spiritually *covers* His servants and handmaids. The Spiritual Master directs these *slaves* of God. In addition, the sons and daughters who are still under the spiritual authority of their fathers can now prophesy. When these sons become young men they now will receive spiritual instructions or visions from God. The old men will also receive dreams to help lead them and those under them. Now these dreams and visions will probably not be as dramatic as those received by Joseph (Mary's husband), but they will receive them. The emphasis being a direct link to God through the Holy

Spirit. There is a direct communication to each individual here. Except for the woman or wife. Why?

Ephesians 5:22-24 "Wives, submit yourselves unto your own husbands, as unto the Lord. For the husband is the head of the wife, even as Christ is the head of the church: and he is the saviour of the body. Therefore as the church is subject unto Christ, so let the wives be to their own husbands in every thing."

Remember, these instructions were given after the event of Pentecost. This is why the woman or wife is not listed. The husband must fulfill his responsibility to be the head of the wife. This is directly related to the curse given in the Garden of Eden. This curse given to the woman (and to the man) was not replaced by Pentecost. It is still in effect.

Isaiah 32:9-12 "Rise up, ye women that are at ease; hear my voice, ye careless daughters; give ear unto my speech. Many days and years shall ye be troubled, ye careless women: for the vintage shall fail, the gathering shall not come. Tremble, ye women that are at ease; be troubled, ye careless ones: strip you, and make you bare, and gird sackcloth upon your loins. They shall lament for the teats, for the pleasant fields, for the fruitful vine."

Many teachers place this warning from Isaiah before the birth of Christ. That may be true. It is describing the spiritual state of women in the nation of Israel. I offer this verse because of the warning Jesus gave to the women who were weeping for him on the road to Calgary. Whenever the woman's natural function of having children is looked upon in a negative way and is pointed out to us as a warning, we know Biblically that soon God will intervene. It is interesting that today, Birth control and Abortions are becoming accepted choices for the woman. She no longer needs to be burdened by having children. If one is barren or if one never has a child today it can be looked upon as a Blessing instead of a curse.

WORSHIPPED THE CREATURE

When trying to understand the importance of God's spiritual roles for men and women, Romans chapter one is a good example of how this is connected to the 'Wrath of God'. Paul writes "To all that be in Rome, beloved of God." We begin with verse 15.

Romans 1:15-16 "So, as much as in me is, I am ready to preach the gospel to you that are at Rome also. For I am not ashamed of the gospel of Christ: for it is the power of God unto salvation to every one that believeth; to the Jew first, and also to the Greek."

Power #1411 force (lit or fig); specifically miraculous power (usually by implication a miracle itself) [from 1410 of uncertain affix; to be able or possible]

The Gospel of Christ is the miraculous power of God unto salvation to every one that believeth.

This power confronts the *spiritual part* of mankind. There is a reaction in the spirit of man to this force of God. It will cause righteousness to be revealed.

Romans 1:17 "For therein is the righteousness of God revealed from faith to faith: as it is written, The just shall live by faith."

Revealed #601 to take off the cover, i.e. disclose

The power of the Holy Spirit is revealed in the Children of God. Faith is part of this action. This is an ongoing process, as the spirit of man is continually fed this energy.

At the same time, this force of the Holy Spirit interacts with the spirit part of the unsaved. As we observe the faithfulness of the saved, we can also view the lack of it from those who are not.

Romans 1:18 "For the wrath of God is revealed from heaven against all ungodliness and unrighteousness of men, who hold the truth in unrighteousness;"

Wrath #3709 properly desire (as a reaching forth or excitement of the mind), i.e. (by analogy) violent passion (ire, or {justifiable} abhorrence); by implication punishment [from 3713 to stretch oneself, i.e. reach out after (long for)]

God's desire is revealed from heaven. This is in the form of a punishment on those who hold the truth in unrighteousness. He has reached out and manipulated with that person's heart and mind. That person's heart and mind will now *reflect* the spiritual wrath they have received from God. This will become a *sign* to the world through their physical behavior. We can see this 'Wrath of God' on an individual today just as well as they could in times past. This is a sign from God (revealed from Heaven) to *mark* them.

Romans 1:19 "Because that which may be known of God is manifest in them; for God hath shewed it unto them."

Manifest #5319 to render apparent (lit. or fig.) [from 5318 shining, apparent, publicly]

God tells us here that they know of Him because "God hath shewed it unto them." How does He place this knowledge in them? From His Spirit into the person's spirit. He makes aware "that which may be known" of Him. This is how it is manifested in a individual.

Romans 1:20 "For the invisible things of him from the creation of the world are clearly seen, being understood by the things that are made, even his eternal power and Godhead; so that they are without excuse:"

Understood #3539 to exercise the mind (observe), i.e. to comprehend, heed [from 3563 the intellect, i.e. the mind, by implication meaning]

Excuse #379 Indefensible [from 1 (as a neg. particle) First & a presumed derivative of 626 give an account (legal plea) of oneself]

God teaches us here that not only does He put this knowledge in a person, but also that person completely understands what they are seeing. This is why they have no defense, no excuse when being held accountable for having this information. The knowledge of the Godhead is placed in them. And the knowledge of Him is also everywhere they look. From inside and outside, they can witness the creation of God. This is clearly seen. This individual weighs this evidence placed in their heart. A spiritual decision is made within.

Romans 1:21 "Because that, when they knew God, they glorified him not as God, neither were thankful; but became vain in their imaginations, and their foolish heart was darkened."

Knew #1097 a prolonged form of a primary verb; to know (absolutely)

Glorified #1392 to Render (or esteem) Glorious [from 1391 Glory (as very apparent)]

Vain #3154 to render foolish, wicked or idolatrous [fr 3152 empty, profitless, or an idol]

Imaginations #1261 Discussion, i.e. (internal) consideration, purpose, debate [from 1260 to reckon thoroughly, to deliberate]

Heart #2588 the heart, i.e. (fig) the thoughts or feelings (mind), also the middle

Darkened #4654 to obscure [from 4655 shadiness, i.e. obscurity]

Having established that these people have been given spiritual knowledge of their Creator, (they *knew* God absolutely) they were expected to glorify God. They did not do this nor were thankful to Him. That person chose a behavior that brought a reaction from God (or a judgment) on their mind and heart. They "glorified him not as God" in their mind, and "neither were thankful" in their heart. Because they did not glorify him (in the mind) they became "vain in their imagination." Because they are not thankful (in the heart) the "foolish heart is darkened." The process of that person's complete spiritual destruction has begun. Note that this language seems to describe the state of the heart and mind of those right before the flood of Noah's day.

Genesis 6:5 "And GOD saw that the wickedness of man was great in the earth, and that every imagination of the thoughts of his heart was only evil continually."

These people *knew* God. Lamech, the father of Noah was alive at the same time as Adam. And yet, the hearts of those people were only producing evil (out of the man's heart, evil thoughts became evil actions). "And the earth was filled with violence through them." They did not glorify God as Noah did. They neither were thankful.

Romans 1:22-23 "Professing themselves to be wise, they became fools, And changed the glory of the uncorruptible God into an image made like to corruptible man, and to birds, and fourfooted beasts, and creeping things."

Who is professing themselves to be wise? Who does God call a fool in this verse?

Romans 1:18 "For the wrath of God is revealed from heaven against all ungodliness and unrighteousness of men, who hold the truth in unrighteousness;"

I believe that these verses are directed at those in a position of Spiritual authority, to the men of God who lead their Church and Congregations. To the Father who is the Spiritual leader of his children, and to the Husband who is the Spiritual leader of his wife. They are held accountable for their spiritual actions. So these men changed the glory of the uncorruptible God into an image utilizing man, birds, beasts, and creeping things.

Genesis 6:7 "And the LORD said, I will destroy man whom I have created from the face of the earth; both man, and beast, and the creeping thing, and the fowls of the air; for it repenteth me that I have made them."

It is interesting that God makes a clean sweep of the man and all his *spiritual toys*. The man's dominion over them was spiritual as well as in a literal way. As always, mankind eventually makes images of them. And he makes the representation in his own likeness.

Image #1504 a likeness, i.e. (lit) statue, profile, or (fig) representation, resemblance [from 1503 a primary verb; to resemble]

This *image* is primary a spiritual image that comes from the heart and mind of that person. This is what they choose to worship. It begins within their heart and mind. The next step is to create a earthly physical representation of these thoughts of their heart.

So what is this *glory* of the uncorruptible God that was changed into an image?

Glory #1391 glory (as very apparent) in a wide application (literally or figuratively, objectively or subjectively) [from the base of 1380 a prolonged form of a primary verb, to think; by implication to seem (truthfully or uncertainly)]

We are given a clue in Romans 1:21

"Because that, when they knew God, they glorified him not as God"

And we are given a clue in Romans 1:25

"Who changed the truth of God into a lie, and worshipped and served the creature more than the Creator"

Is glory a state of belief? Thinking seems to be part of the process. Is the Truth of God part of this glory? In John we read that the glory of the Christ is full of grace and truth.

John 1:14 "And the Word was made flesh, and dwelt among us, (and we beheld his glory, the glory as of the only begotten of the Father,) full of grace and truth."

Truth is part of this glory. And Jesus Christ brought the Truth of God to the world.

John 18:37 "Pilate therefore said unto him, Art thou a king then? Jesus answered, Thou sayest that I am a king. To this end was I born, and for this cause came I into the world, that I should bear witness unto the truth. Every one that is of the truth heareth my voice."

"For this cause came I into the world." Jesus our King bears witness of the truth to the world. The Kings that are saved by God are also to witness the Truth to the world. Those who God anoints. Many are not 'anointed' by God. That is the problem here in Romans.

2 Corinthians 8:23 "Whether any do enquire of Titus, he is my partner and fellowhelper concerning you: or our brethren be enquired of, they are the messengers of the churches, and the glory of Christ."

The messengers of the churches are the glory of Christ. Their *message* is Jesus Christ. They witness for the truth. They are sent by God to do a job. To give God glory through the works they do. Not human works, but the *spiritual works* that is accomplished.

2 Thessalonians 1:10 "When he shall come to be glorified in his saints, and to be admired in all them that believe (because our testimony among you was believed) in that day."

Christ is *glorified* in his saints and to be admired in all them that believe. So we can see that the testimony of the truth of Christ is part of this process of glory.

Hebrews 2:10 "For it became him, for whom are all things, and by whom are all things, in bringing many sons unto glory, to make the captain of their salvation perfect through sufferings."

Many sons are brought unto glory. And these sons that suffer for it are the glory of God.

1 Peter 4:14 "If ye be reproached for the name of Christ, happy are ye; for the spirit of glory and of God resteth upon you: on their part he is evil spoken of, but on your part he is glorified."

Persecution for Christ's name means the Holy Spirit (the spirit of glory) rests upon you. This is how the sons *glorify* Christ. So we see that the Glory of God is connected to those who are given spiritual rule. And Spiritual rulers must always follow the truth.

1 Corinthians 11:7 "For a man indeed ought not to cover his head, forasmuch as he is the image and glory (#1391) of God: but the woman is the glory (#1391) of the man."

It says here that the man is the image and glory of God. It also states that the woman is the glory of the man. The man here is connected to the glory of God. He is created in a way that makes him responsible (created spiritually responsible) for the Truth of God. Especially over his own household, his wife (in which God joins them together), and all of his children (given by God to him). Now, back to these men in Romans.

Romans 1:22-23 "Professing themselves to be wise, they became fools, And changed the glory of the uncorruptible God into an image made like to corruptible man, and to birds, and fourfooted beasts, and creeping things."

These men in spiritual authority (who thought they were wise like the sons of God) changed the glory of the incorruptible God (the Truth of God, Jesus Christ) into an image that came from their own heart and mind and presented this to the world for their own glory. They wanted followers to have a like mind. A corruptible mind just like theirs.

Corruptible #5349 decayed, (by implication) perishable [from 5351 shrivel, spoil, ruin]

The Truth of the God-man (Jesus Christ) was changed into an image of the self-man.

Romans 1:24 "Wherefore God also gave them up to uncleanness through the lusts of their own hearts, to dishonour their own bodies between themselves:"

Gave up, Gave over #3860 to Surrender, i.e. yield up, intrust, transmit [from 3844 near, from, beside, or at the vicinity of (beyond or opposed to) & 1325 to give]

We will find that God gives them up to vile affections and gives them over to a reprobate mind. We read of the heart and mind of mankind again. How does God give them up?

The biggest clue is in the word uncleanness. It is this person's final spiritual state.

Uncleanness #167 impurity (the quality), physically or morally [from 169 impure which is from #1 (as a negative particle) and a presumed derivative of 2508 to cleanse, i.e. (specifically) to prune; figuratively to expiate]

When God surrenders or yields up His Will on a individual over a contested heart and mind issue, the result is that the person will fall away from the Truth. God stops *pruning* that branch. Note that this is a Spiritual action. This will cause a spiritual reaction from the one affected. That person's lust of the heart will direct his body from now on.

Lusts #1939 a longing (especially for what is forbidden) [from 1937 to set the heart upon]

Heart #2588 the Heart, i.e. (fig) the thoughts or feelings (mind); also the middle

Romans 1:24 "Wherefore God also gave them up to uncleanness through the lusts of their own hearts, to dishonour their own bodies between themselves:"

So God stops his pruning (in the spirit of that person) and uncleanness is the result. This is achieved through the Heart. The spirit now unrestrained, lusts after things that are forbidden. Like the woman in the Garden of Eden, she wanted to be wiser but instead was foolish. Her heart (desires) led her to dishonour her own body Adam, or the one flesh.

So, how does one "dishonour their own bodies between themselves" in this passage?

Dishonour #818 to render infamous, i.e. (by implication) contemn or maltreat [from 820 unhonoured]

Bodies #4983 the Body (as a sound whole), used in a very wide application, literal or figurative [from 4982 to save, i.e. deliver or protect (literally or figuratively]

Between #1722 a primary prep. denoting (fixed) position (in place, time, or state), and by implication instrumentality (medially or constructively), i.e. a relation of rest; "in", at, (up-), on, by, etc

Themselves #1438 from a reflexive pronoun otherwise obsolete And the general (dative [case] or accusative [case]) of [846 the reflexive pronoun self] him- (her-, it-, them-, also (in conjunction with the personal pronoun of the other persons) my-, thy-, our-, your-) self (selves), etc.

The longing of the self-reality is allowed by God to direct that man's heart. They have made a spiritual image of the self to worship. But we must worship God's spirit.

John 4:24 "God is a Spirit: and they that worship him must worship him in spirit and in truth."

These men are in violation of this verse. No worshipping in truth or in spirit. Their bodies have become dishonoured. And those they spiritually lead are also dishonoured.

Ephesians 5:23 "For the husband is the head of the wife, even as Christ is the head of the church: and he is the saviour of the body (#4983)."

Saviour #4990 a Deliverer, i.e. God or Christ [from 4982 to save, deliver, protect]

In the book of Ephesians chapter 5, we read that the husband and wife is a picture of Christ and His church. In verses 25 to 27, husbands are given instructions to love their wives as Christ loved the church. Bring the Truth. Witness for the Truth. Live the Truth.

Ephesians 5:28-29 "So ought men to love their wives as their own bodies. He that loveth his wife loveth himself. For no man ever yet hated his own flesh; but nourisheth and cherisheth it, even as the Lord the church:"

These passages are offered because they help to identify whom God is referencing in the Roman verses. Paul is warning the Church in Rome about those who hold the truth in unrighteousness. Those who knew God. Who desired to be wise. And who taught the Judgment of God. These are men, not women. The word *bodies* in Romans 1:24 is speaking about the man and wife (one flesh) as well as those men who were not married.

Mark 10:8 "And they twain shall be one flesh: so then they are no more twain, but one flesh."

The body is dishonoured. The man is commanded to honor the weaker vessel.

1 Peter 3:7 "Likewise, ye husbands, dwell with them according to knowledge, giving honour unto the wife, as unto the weaker vessel, and as being heirs together of the grace of life; that your prayers be not hindered."

He is not to dishonor his own body (being heirs together of the grace of life). This will hinder or cut off their prayers to God. Remember, God spiritually ties them together.

Romans 1:25 "Who changed the truth of God into a lie, and worshipped and served the creature more than the Creator, who is blessed for ever. Amen."

This is a very interesting passage. These 'fools' took the Truth of God (Jesus Christ who is the Way, the Truth, and the Life) and changed this message into a lie. They then served the creature more than the Creator. The Strong's concordance describes this action as to '**venerate** and **minister** the creature more than the creator'. It is commonly taught that the Creator is God and the creature (or creation) is the Earth including mankind depending on who is teaching. Is this a correct conclusion? Just who is the Creator and creature in this verse?

Creator #2936 to Fabricate, i.e. found (form original) [probably akin to {2932 a primary verb; to get, i.e. acquire} (through the idea of proprietorship of the manufacturer) to get, i.e. acquire (by any means; own)]

When we look at the word Creator, we see that it is active. It 'fabricates', it 'acquires'. This action (in a spiritual setting) creates the creature. It has proprietorship.

Creature #2937 original formation (properly the act; by implication the thing, literally or figuratively) [from 2936]

Colossians 1:15-18 "Who is the image of the invisible God, the firstborn of every creature: For by him were all things created, that are in heaven, and that are in earth, visible and invisible, whether they be thrones, or dominions, or principalities, or powers: all things were created by him, and for him: And he is before all things, and by him all things consist. And he is the head of the body, the church: who is the beginning, the firstborn from the dead; that in all things he might have the preeminence."

The Creator is identified in these Colossians passages. We read, "For by him were all things created." He is the firstborn (form original), the head of the body, the church. We are to worship and serve Christ (glorify Him). God uses the words Creator and creation to focus us on the spiritual aspect that is going on in these Romans verses. Remember, we are talking about the Truth of God being changed into a lie. The message of Salvation changed into a message of self-glory that brings no salvation. So, who are these creatures that are served? If Christ is the firstborn of every creature (form original), and this is a Spiritual Birth, then the creatures (original formation) are those made in His Image.

James 1:18 "Of his own will begat he us with the word of truth, that we should be a kind of firstfruits of his creatures."

John 1:12-13 "But as many as received him, to them gave he power to become the sons of God, even to them that believe on his name: Which were born, not of blood, nor of the will of the flesh, nor of the will of man, but of God."

These verses explain (and help us focus on the spiritual aspect of what is being taught) who the creature is. The creature is the representation of the Creator here on Earth. These creatures placed themselves above the Truth of God (they changed this truth into a lie).

They changed the *Glory* of God to the *glory* of man. They served themselves. Those who are under their spiritual authority were taught this lie. They were led away from the Truth of God.

Romans 1:26 "For this cause God gave them up unto vile affections: for even their women did change the natural use into that which is against nature:"

Vile #819 infamy, i.e. (subjectively) comparative indignity, (objectively) disgrace [from 820 (negatively) unhonoured or (positively) dishonoured]

Affections #3806 properly suffering ("pathos") i.e. (subjectively) a passion (especially concupiscence) [from the alternate of 3958 to experience a sensation or impression]

This verse is commonly taught that these vile affections are a desire for homosexuality. The next verse talks about burning lust and men with men. Some also teach that the recompence of their error is AIDS (God is punishing them for this sexual practice.) Is this what God is teaching in this verse? Did He suddenly stop teaching Spiritual *things*? The biggest problem I have with the homosexual curse teaching is that everything we have been reading seems to apply to ALL. ALL men are given the knowledge of God (His eternal power and Godhead.) ALL that glorified him not as God had their foolish heart darkened. ALL are given up to uncleanness. ALL dishonour their own bodies. ALL are given up to vile affections. ALL begin to want other men sexually? Really? And do ALL of their women also want other females sexually now? Or do we stop applying the all at this point? Many teachers do just that. They ignore the fact that this is for ALL.

I see *suffering* here for that person. Suffering that is described as infamy or disgraced. This is a spiritual suffering. The crime was spiritual, the punishment is spiritual. Our spirit isn't ignored in this re-directing of desires. It is the most important part of us. Any action from God to us will always affect us as a whole. God will always re-direct us first in our spirit. So when these bodies (or the one flesh) are given up to vile affections, this will show itself in their women. They will *reflect* their spiritual leader.

Romans 1:26 "For this cause God gave them up unto vile affections: for even their women did change the natural (#5446) use into that which is against nature (5449):"

The question here is what is the natural use of the woman? The spiritual natural use?

NATURAL (N.T.)

#1083 gennesis, nativity (not the nativity word itself which is #4128) [from 1080 to procreate (properly of the father, but by extension of the mother); fig. to regenerate]

James 1:23 (1 time used) "…he is like unto a man beholding his natural face in a glass"

In the New Testament, (#1083) we can have double meanings (spiritual, physical). A hearer of the Word and not a doer is deceived. A man who sees his natural state of being (a spiritually dead self) reflected back, ends up deceived and thinks he is a doer. Used here in James, the natural state of a person is an unsaved soul.

#5446 physical i.e. (by impl.) instinctive [from 5449 growth (by germination or expansion), i.e. (by impl.) natural production (lineal descent); by extension a genus or sort; fig. native disposition, constitution or usage]

This #5446 is in Rom 1:26-27 and in 2 Pet 2:12.

Rom 1:26 "...their women did change the natural use into that which is against nature."
Rom 1:27 "...likewise also the men, leaving the natural use of the woman"
2 Pet 2:12 "But these, as natural brute beasts, made to be taken and destroyed..."

(#5446) says physical or instinctive. This physical or instinctive natural is identified by growth. Growth of linage or genus or sort. Growth of disposition, constitution (laws).

Because 2 of the 3 examples from the Bible say natural use. We need to look at use.

Use #5540 employment, i.e. (spec.) sexual intercourse (as an occupation of the body) [from 5530 a primary verb; to furnish what is needed; (give an oracle, "graze" [touch slightly], light upon, etc.), i.e. .by implication to employ or (by extension) to act toward one in a given manner]

God *employed* the woman to be heirs together of the grace of life with her husband. A warning is given about 'hindering their prayers'. The woman is to submit (spiritually) to her husband as unto the Lord. She is to get her spiritual guidance and answers from him. These are the duties of a spiritual helpmet. This is the natural way to function spiritually.

Physically, women were to be a helpmeet (in everything) and to raise children to love and obey God. This is their natural physical use. Spiritually, the woman's desire is to their husband. He is to rule over them. This is the natural spiritual use. The context in the Romans passages is talking about ALL who hold the Truth in unrighteousness. ALL have changed the natural use against nature. And we must include the 2 Pet 2:12 passage also.

#5591 sensitive, i.e. animate (in distinction on the one hand from 4152, which is the higher or renovated nature, and on the other from 5446, which is the lower or bestial nature)

This #5591 is found in 1 Cor 2:14 & 1 Cor 15:44, 46.

1 Cor 2:14 "But the <u>natural</u> man receiveth not the things of the Spirit of God..."
1 Cor 15:44 "It is sown a <u>natural</u> body; it is raised a spiritual body. There is a <u>natural</u> body, and a spiritual body"
1 Cor 15:46 "...but that which is <u>natural</u>; and afterward that which is spiritual."

(#5591) directs us to the physical aspect of natural. The definition itself (sensitive and animate) identifies with the flesh. Even the 3 verses that are used, show us two different bodies. A spiritual body and a natural body (both in the same person).

A natural spiritual and physical *use*. How does this fit in with the meaning of Nature?

NATURE (N.T.)
#1078 genesis, nativity (not the nativity word itself which is #4128), figuratively nature [from the same as 1074 a generation; by implication an age (the period or the persons)]

James 3:6 (1 time) "...and setteth on fire the course of <u>nature</u>; and it is set on fire of hell"

Figuratively nature. Course of figurative nature. Spiritually, a Heaven or Hell direction for the person involved. The tongue is the sail of this ship. The nature of the self.

#5449 Growth (by germination or expansion), i.e. (by impl.) natural production (lineal descent); by extension a genus or sort; fig. native disposition, constitution or usage [from 5453 to puff or blow; swell up, to germinate or grow] (12 uses in Scripture)

While some of these (12) verses imply a literal, physical growth, some of these verses clearly teach a spiritual growth. (And some verses imply or suggest both aspects.)

Rom 2:14 "...which have not the law, do by <u>nature</u> the things contained in the law..."

They show the work of the law written in their hearts. They spiritually obey God.

Rom 11:24 "...wild by <u>nature</u>, and wert grafted contrary to <u>nature</u> into a good olive..."

God is speaking about people here, so the nature cannot be a literal grafting. A group of people spiritually becoming one family. Becoming one with the spiritual olive tree.

Gal 4:8 "...ye knew not God, ye did service unto them which by <u>nature</u> are no gods."

They're not natural gods. They are not spiritually qualified to be gods. Spiritual nature.

Eph 2:3 "...and were by <u>nature</u> the children of wrath, even as others."

We were in an unsaved state of being (nature) once, as were the others. A spiritual nature.

2 Pet 1:4 "...that by these ye might be partakers of the divine nature, having escaped..."

Divine nature. This cannot be physical. A spiritual nature. Divine (#2304) means godlike.

Genesis 3:16 "Unto the woman he said, I will greatly multiply thy sorrow and thy conception; in sorrow thou shalt bring forth children; and thy desire shall be to thy husband, and he shall rule over thee."

This verse in Genesis shows us the natural use, the spiritual natural use of woman. We need each other to serve God in a way that pleases Him. This spiritual system God created benefits both partners. God's headship with its Spiritual Covering is *natural.* Now, when you change the Truth of God into a lie, and worship anything other than the Creator, there is a spiritual price to pay WHILE YOU ARE VISITING EARTH! This spiritual punishment is happening to them now. While they live. And we can see this.

Romans 1:18 "For the wrath of God is revealed from heaven against all ungodliness and unrighteousness of men, who hold the truth in unrighteousness;"

One more note on the natural use of the woman. Physically the natural use is this. To have children (Gen 9:1) and to avoid fornication (1 Cor 7:2-5). I'm sure that many of these people continued to have children and still avoided fornication as before. Without the spiritual understanding (comparing spiritual things with spiritual) and the application to the verses we read here, the teaching becomes a homosexual issue.

God has now re-directed their desires. The woman does not want the spiritual rule of the man. Their desire now resembles Eve's desire to be wiser. And how the men.

Romans 1:27a "And likewise also the men, leaving the natural use of the woman, burned in their lust (#3715) one toward another;"

Burned #1572 to inflame deeply [from 1537 origin and 2545 primary verb; to set on fire]

Lust #3715 excitement of the mind, i.e. longing after [from 3713 to stretch oneself, i.e. reach out after (long for)]

If the women no longer desire the headship, neither do the men. They leave the natural use of the woman and look to men to spiritually lead them and be their covering. This verse is generally taught that this is a lust for homosexually. The problem with this is that this Lust is #3715 and not Lust #1939. We see this in 1 John 2:16-17 very clearly. #1939 is the Lust of the flesh, a longing, especially for what is forbidden.

1 John 2:16-17 "Love not the world, neither the things that are in the world. If any man love the world, the love of the Father is not in him. For all that is in the world, the lust (#1939) of the flesh, and the lust (#1939) of the eyes, and the pride of life, is not of the Father, but is of the world. And the world passeth away, and the lust (#1939) thereof: but he that doeth the will of God abideth for ever."

Remember that these men (and the one flesh) are under the Wrath (or desire) of God.

Wrath #3709 properly desire (as a reaching forth or <u>excitement of the mind</u>), i.e. (by analogy) violent passion (ire, or [justifiable] abhorrence); by implication punishment [from 3713 to stretch oneself, i.e. reach out after (long for)]

God's tinkering with that person (<u>excitement of the mind</u>) changes the spiritual desires within that person. The Wrath of God comes with active punishment. This means that while that person still lives they are redirected in the heart and mind. God sets the course for that person's life and uses them to further His Salvation plan.

Romans 1:27b "...men with men working that which is unseemly,"

Working #2716 do work fully, i.e. accomplish; by implication to finish, fashion [from 2596 down (in place or time) and 2038 to toil (as a task, occupation, etc,); (by implication) effect, be engaged in or with, etc.]

Unseemly #808 an indecency; by implication the pudenda [from 809 prop. shapeless, i.e. (fig) inelegant]

Men with men working. A group of men like the Pharisees? New Testament Pharisees?

New Testament teachers? These men who hold the truth in unrighteousness still show up for work. They still are leading others away from the Truth. Because God has given them up, their *works* are fashioned or set. These works result in something that God calls unseemly or an indecency. It is a picture of the church that has no spiritual covering from God. They are in a spiritual way naked. And nakedness needs a covering.

Genesis 2:24-25 "Therefore shall a man leave his father and his mother, and shall cleave unto his wife: and they shall be one flesh. And they were both naked, the man and his wife, and were not ashamed."

God tells us that this is a picture of the church. Here we can be naked but not ashamed because God is the head of Christ, and Christ is the head of the man, and the man is the head of the woman. This order was changed for these persons and their one flesh.

Today's society really reflects these changed desires in almost all men and all women.

Romans 1:27c "...and receiving in themselves that recompence of their error which was meet."

Recompence #489 Requital, Correspondence [from a comparison of 473 opposite, i.e. instead or because of & 3408 a primary word; pay for services (good or bad)]

Error #4106 (obj.) fraudulence, (subj.) a straying from orthodoxy or piety [feminine of 4108 (as abstract roving (as a tramp), i.e. (by implication) an impostor or misleader]

You notice that the recompence is directed at the men. Yes, both sexes are given to vile affections, but God is cursing the spiritual headship of the men. In 1 Corinthians 11:3 God tells us that the head of every man is Christ and the head of the woman is the man. This natural headship is now *unnatural.* When God says that these men receive the recompence of their error, He is saying that they received the same error (fraudulence) they sowed in those spiritually under them. Now lets review the last 2 Roman verses.

Romans 1:26-27 "For this cause God gave them up unto vile affections:

(Spiritual suffering that is vile, dishonoring to their flesh and called infamy by God)

for even their women did change the natural use into that which is against nature:

(The natural spiritual use is desires given to us from God during the curse in Eden)

And likewise also the men, leaving the natural use of the woman,

(Men are to rule over their wife, to be the natural spiritual leader of the women)

burned in their lust one toward another;

(These men desired above all else [burned in their lust] to be the covering of other men)

men with men working that which is unseemly,

(Men with men are the *Beast.* They accomplish an indecency-the nakedness of spirit)

and receiving in themselves that recompence of their error which was meet."

(Their headship was wrong so their punishment matches their crime)

Remember, God uses Adultery (a sexual reference) to teach us about spiritual rebellion to Him. He also uses the term vile affections here in the same way. (As a sexual reference.) Lets look at the two punishments given to those professing to be wise. He will give them up to uncleanness through the lusts of their own heart and give them over to a reprobate mind. Romans 1:21 show us another description of what is happening.

Romans 1:21 "Because that, when they knew God, they glorified him not as God, neither were thankful; but became vain in their imaginations, and their foolish heart was darkened."

First we will look at the heart. It is a very bad thing when someone's foolish heart is darkened. This heart is not a literal heart that becomes a darker color. The heart and the spirit of man are tied together. In the heart (our thoughts or feelings) we will find that person's real relationship to God. Our spirit (which is connected to God's Spirit) is our only source of spiritual truth in this world. When God darkens our heart, we lose sight of the Truth. He is withdrawing more of his *presence* and *restraint* in that person. He allows that soul to become more and more unclean. The soul draws farther and farther away from God and from the Truth. This person's heart will now provide the justification for sin in whatever the reprobate mind desires. The heart and mind now serve the 'Self'. But the hearts of these (wise fools) must be first given up by God. Then the direction of their heart is set. The Bible talks extensively about our heart and mind. Jesus teaches that out of the heart of men proceed evil thoughts. So the person's heart must be altered first.

Mark 7:21-23 "For from within, out of the heart of men, proceed evil thoughts, adulteries, fornications, murders, Thefts, covetousness, wickedness, deceit, lasciviousness, an evil eye, blasphemy, pride, foolishness: All these evil things come from within, and defile the man."

We will see a similar list of these sins in Romans 1:29-31. But back to these men.

Vile Affections = Spiritual Judgment. Reprobate Mind = Physical Judgment.

Now that the heart of this person desires complete idolatry, God completes the process.

Romans 1:28a "And even as they did not like to retain God in their knowledge,"

Retain #2192 a primary verb; to hold (various applications, lit. or fig., direct or remote; such as possession; ability, contiguity, relation, or condition)

Knowledge #1922 Recognition, i.e. (by implication) full discernment, acknowledgement [from 1921 to know upon some mark, i.e. recognize; become fully acquainted with]

They did not walk with God to say the least. Honest Christians can understand what is happening here. There are many times we do not like to retain what God teaches us, both within and/or around us. Some of this knowledge demands action or obedience. But these men in Romans changed the glory of the uncorruptible God into corruptible images. So…

Romans 1:28b "God gave them over to a reprobate mind,"

Gave up, Gave over #3860 to Surrender, i.e. yield up, intrust, transmit [from 3844 near, from, beside, or at the vicinity of (beyond or opposed to) & 1325 to give]

Reprobate #96 Unapproved, i.e. rejected, (by implication) worthless [from 1 first (as a neg. particle) & 1384 acceptable, i.e. approved]

Mind #3563 the intellect, i.e. mind (divine or human; in thought, feeling, or will); by implication: meaning [probably from the base of 1097 to know (absolutely)]

Again God takes an action on this person. The heart and mind that is given up by God is on its own. This person will never have the Mind of Christ. This is total free will.

Romans 1:28c "... to do those things which are not convenient;"

Convenient #2520 to reach to, i.e. becoming [from 2596 Down (in place or time) & 2240 a primary verb to arrive, i.e. be present (lit. or fig.)]

These men did not like to retain God in their knowledge. Because they are vain in their imagination, God has no place in them. There is no Truth in them. This allows for a reprobate mind to take over. This reprobate mind will direct a path for the self. It is in a survivor mode. This person can now produce the anti-fruits for the anti-spirit. In other words, when a man believes that God is 'this' and in spiritual reality God is 'not this', he has used his imagination to lead himself to do evil continually. Because the heart is darkened and the mind is reprobate, this individual is now wide open to committing many grievous sins.

Romans 1:29-31 "Being filled with all unrighteousness, fornication, wickedness, covetousness, maliciousness; full of envy, murder, debate, deceit, malignity; whisperers, Backbiters, haters of God, despiteful, proud, boasters, inventors of evil things, disobedient to parents, Without understanding, covenantbreakers, without natural affection, implacable, unmerciful:"

This describes an individual who is building their own kingdom of Heaven. He is the god of his own heart and mind that was supposed to serve and obey the LORD.

2 Peter 2:1 "But there were false prophets also among the people, even as there shall be false teachers among you, who privily shall bring in damnable heresies, even denying the Lord that bought them, and bring upon themselves swift destruction."

This letter to the Romans brings a serious warning to all Christians in Spiritual Authority. There is a responsibility of knowledge here. We know in our spirit that God wants us to live by faith. Our heart and mind know what God requires of us. We are to glorify God.

Romans 1:32 "Who knowing the judgment of God, that they which commit such things are worthy of death, not only do the same, but have pleasure in them that do them."

Bound By The Law

Romans 7:1 "Know ye not, brethren, (for I speak to them that know the law,) how that the law hath dominion over a man as long as he liveth?"

Paul sends a legal brief (under the inspiration of the Holy Spirit) to the church in Rome. He opens with a statement that both can agree upon. The Law has dominion over a man as long as he lives. He then goes on to explain how this law affects the *one flesh*.

Romans 7:2 "For the woman which hath an husband is bound by the law to her husband so long as he liveth; but if the husband be dead, she is loosed from the law of her husband."

This Law has dominion over the woman also. God is very serious about the marriage institution and scripted special ordinances if there was ever a divorce between the Husband and the Wife. Consider:

Ezekiel 16:38 "And I will judge thee, as women that break wedlock and shed blood are judged; and I will give thee blood in fury and jealousy."

In the Romans passage we read "the woman which hath an husband is bound by the law to her Husband." This *binding* law for the wife originated in the Old Testament.

Deuteronomy 24:1 "When a man hath taken a wife, and married her, and it come to pass that she find no favour in his eyes, because he hath found some uncleanness in her: then let him write her a bill of divorcement, and give it in her hand, and send her out of his house."

Jesus refined this law given in Deuteronomy during the Sermon on the Mount.

Matthew 5:31-32 "It hath been said, Whosoever shall put away his wife, let him give her a writing of divorcement: But I say unto you, That whosoever shall put away his wife, saving for the cause of fornication, causeth her to commit adultery: and whosoever shall marry her that is divorced committeth adultery."

Note that only the men were allowed to divorce their wives for fornication. The woman had no such option, and this was also the *law*. This decree was well known, as Paul uses the example of marriage in this Romans passage to illustrate the strength of the law.

Romans 7:3 "So then if, while her husband liveth, she be married to another man, she shall be called an adulteress: but if her husband be dead, she is free from that law; so that she is no adulteress, though she be married to another man."

The life or death of the husband determined the physical and spiritual freedom of the wife. Once again, we see the Spiritual headship taught here. The wife is bound to her husband and under his headship as long as he lives. If the woman marries another man while her first husband still lives, the *covering* of the first husband is violated. She is now called an adulteress. What is this covering? And why is it placed over the woman?

1 Corinthians 11:3 "But I would have you know, that the head of every man is Christ; and the head of the woman is the man; and the head of Christ is God."

This covering on the woman is the spiritual headship given to the man. It is a pecking order of spiritual authority. This doesn't change in a divorce. An example of this spiritual headship is found in the Book of Luke. God appointed all things to Christ who then in turn appoints to His Apostles a kingdom. God delegates this spiritual administration.

Luke 22:29 "And I appoint unto you a kingdom, as my Father hath appointed unto me;"

God has also delegated an authority to the husband. It is a spiritual responsibility over the wife. What is this spiritual authority? And what is the responsibility that accompanies it?

Ephesians 5:23-24 "For the husband is the head of the wife, even as Christ is the head of the church: and he is the saviour of the body. Therefore as the church is subject unto Christ, so let the wives be to their own husbands in every thing."

Why would God make this comparison? The husband is the head of the wife even as Christ as the head of the Church. Christ guides us into truth to keep us safe from false teachers and false *christs*. Does the husband serve here in a similar way?

1 Corinthians 11:10 "For this cause ought the woman to have power on her head because of the angels."

This is explained in more detail in the chapter "The covering of a woman." When a woman (who still has a spiritual covering from her 1st husband) goes and marries another man (who also gives her a spiritual covering) she becomes a spiritual adulteress. She is placing herself under another *covering*. And yet, if the first husband dies, his covering for her is gone. She is free from that law. She now has only the covering of her new husband. She is not an adulteress now, though she is married to another man. Spiritual headship is an integral part of the man/woman relationship. And this relationship is meant to serve Almighty God; therefore He set these rules in us and in Scripture for His purpose. Today, nobody seems to be 'Bound' to anything. The headship in Scripture and how it is applied in a marriage are a distant if not forgotten practice, much less viewed as a Law from God.

Romans 7:4 "Wherefore, my brethren, ye also are become dead to the law by the body of Christ; that ye should be married to another, even to him who is raised from the dead, that we should bring forth fruit unto God."

With this example of a marriage under the law, we can apply this to our understanding of verse 4. We were spiritually married to the Law. Our soul is under this law. If we were found guilty, it was death for our soul. The Law was our husband and we were bound to it as long as we live. When Christ paid for the sins of the Elect (by the body of Christ), we became free from that law.

Christ died and so now the law died to us. We are now free to marry Jesus Christ, and through that union, produce the fruit of the Spirit to God's Glory. But the Law isn't done with us. We are now under the Law of Christ.

Galatians 6:2 "Bear ye one another's burdens, and so fulfil the law of Christ."

Jesus told us of these laws in the Gospels. His Apostles expanded upon them in the following books of the Bible. Finally in the Book of Revelation, we can see the result of these laws upon mankind. Even though they are summarized into two laws we must not ignore all of the details given to us in the New Testament.

Mark 12:30-31 "And thou shalt love the Lord thy God with all thy heart, and with all thy soul, and with all thy mind, and with all thy strength: this is the first commandment. And the second is like, namely this, Thou shalt love thy neighbour as thyself. There is none other commandment greater than these."

To sum it up quickly…

The sin of adultery is excused by the death of the husband.

(Mankind's worship of false gods is forgiven by the death of Christ.)

"Ye also are become dead to the law by the body of Christ."

All new sins forgiven (by Christ) despite the law still in existence.

"That ye should be married to another, even to him who is raised from the dead, that we should bring forth fruit unto God."

We leave our old husband (the law) & marry another (Christ) & make spiritual babies (bring forth fruit.)

1 Corinthians 7:39 "The wife is bound by the law as long as her husband liveth; but if her husband be dead, she is at liberty to be married to whom she will; only in the Lord."

1 Corinthians 7:39 teach us that this (bound by the law) is still in effect, after the event of Pentecost when God's Spirit was poured out upon all flesh. These early Churches followed this Law. They took these ordinances very seriously. It is the Word of God to them. The wife is bound to her husband as long as he lives; for physical and spiritual reasons. And the husband is the *head* of the wife. "To the death do us part."

It Is Good For A Man Not To Touch A Woman

This church at Corinth had a lot of questions about marriage, divorce, virgins, and wives.

1 Corinthians 7:1 "Now concerning the things whereof ye wrote unto me: It is good for a man not to touch a woman."

Touch #680 to attach oneself to, i.e. touch (in many applications) [reflexive of 681 to fasten to; to set on fire]

"It is good for a man not to touch a woman." Why would God make this statement? This church had written to Paul regarding numerous sins of the flesh that were prevalent in their congregation. He begins his answer with an incredulous statement. And it seems to go against what Scripture teaches. We know that God created man and woman to go forth and to multiply. He created the marriage bed to be undefiled. (Heb 13:4) We have His permission to enjoy our marriage in our flesh. We must obey God's command to pro-create. But here Paul says that it is good for a man not to touch a woman. Why? The answer is this church had allowed a fleshly distraction to grow within the congregation. It was sexual fornication.

1 Corinthians 5:1 "It is reported commonly that there is fornication among you, and such fornication as is not so much as named among the Gentiles, that one should have his father's wife."

Yes, that means having sex with your mother. But that wasn't the worst part. This church had become tolerant to some of these acts. (5:2) God spells out specific instructions to this congregation for those who were engaged in this. Deliver one to Satan (5:5), purge out (5:7), do not keep company (5:11), and put away from yourselves that wicked person. (5:13) These instructions were meant to bring this church back to walking in the Will of God. Because they changed His command of pro-*creation* to pro-*recreation*, their outward behavior as children of God countered their witnessing of the Gospel message. Paul reminds the congregation that the Holy Spirit dwells within them.

1 Corinthians 6:18-20 "Flee fornication. Every sin that a man doeth is without the body; but he that committeth fornication sinneth against his own body. What? know ye not that your body is the temple of the Holy Ghost which is in you, which ye have of God, and ye are not your own? For ye are bought with a price: therefore glorify God in your body, and in your spirit, which are God's."

These acts of fornication were affecting the *body* as a whole. If you compare the seven Churches in the Book of Revelation and how God describes their spiritual relationship to Him, we can see that this church is close to matching them. We find in later chapters of 1 Corinthians that Paul will remind this church of the spiritual headship in the home (Chapter 11) and in the congregation. (Chapter 14) In this chapter Paul will give basic instructions in how to deal with the fleshly sexual urges.

1 Corinthians 7:2 "Nevertheless, to avoid fornication, let every man have his own wife, and let every woman have her own husband."

Fornication #4202 Harlotry (adultery and incest); fig. Idolatry [from 4203 act, indulge]

The Man and the Woman become one flesh. They share their bodies as if it was not their own. They are to do this to *avoid fornication*. So that Satan cannot tempt you while you have sexual desires. This physical act creates a spiritual defense against the evil one. It is very important, not to be trifled with as what was occurring with these worshipers. Satan will attack you through your physical desires. He doesn't care with whom or how you commit sexual fornication, just that you do. Many who commit such acts become silent witnesses for the evil one. It is difficult to ask others to live according to what the Lord commands when we ourselves do not. If we do not speak up or defend God's Word, this helps Satan attack the church. And as more give in to this desire the mindset of the congregation will eventually twist the Gospel message toward excusing this kind of behavior. To some degree almost all the congregations today have succumbed to this form of spiritual attack.

1 Corinthians 7:3-4 "Let the husband render unto the wife due benevolence: and likewise also the wife unto the husband. The wife hath not power of her own body, but the husband: and likewise also the husband hath not power of his own body, but the wife."

Benevolence #2133 Kindness, conjugal duty [from same as 2132 well-minded, reconcile]

Power #1850 to Control [from 1849 privilege; force; freedom; mastery, influence]

There are several important issues not to be missed in these verses. First of all, God uses the words man and wife. Not man and man, or wife and wife. Secondly, this is talking about sexual acts not necessary for making babies. These sexual acts are to help one avoid committing adultery. And because of this, God sets down some ground rules. He uses the word *benevolence* for both spouses. This is an equal kindness. We make our bodies (that is, bodies that God gave us to do His Will) *available* to our other half. God states that neither spouse has control of his or her own body. He wants us to use this (conjugal duty) as a line of defense against the evil one. Any disruption to this one flesh system can allow Satan to put a foot in the door in any marriage. If any woman or man tells their spouse that it is their right to refuse their partner sex because it is 'my body', they are in rebellion to this verse in Corinthians. They open up their selves to an attack from Satan. Differences in the frequency of the act must be worked out between the couple. What is worked out between them must reflect the wisdom of these verses.

1 Corinthians 7:5 "Defraud ye not one the other, except it be with consent for a time, that ye may give yourselves to fasting and prayer; and come together again, that Satan tempt you not for your incontinency"

Defraud #650 to despoil [from 575 "off", i.e. away (from something near) & {stereo}to deprive]

Here God tells us that this must be worked out between the couple. It is that important. Note that the lack of the act is replaced with fasting and prayer. The spiritual aspect or connection is consistent with or without the act. Both actions defend us from Satan. Do not defraud one another we are told. We must consider this verse when working this out with our partner, our one flesh. This is commanded for the good of the marriage.

1 Corinthians 7:6-9 "But I speak this by permission, and not of commandment. For I would that all men were even as I myself. But every man hath his proper gift of God, one after this manner, and another after that. I say therefore to the unmarried and widows, It is good for them if they abide even as I. But if they cannot contain, let them marry: for it is better to marry than to burn."

Permission by God to speak this is still the Word of God. Paul would like all men to live as he. What does that mean? Paul was concerned about getting the Gospel message out in truth. That is what he is focusing on. Anything else is a distraction in getting that message out. This is what Paul is conveying. If you do not have to marry, don't. Let your focus be on the Kingdom of God. That way you can be the most use to Him. With this said, Paul also tells the unmarried and widows to follow this example if they are able.

1 Corinthians 7:10-11 "And unto the married I command, yet not I, but the Lord, Let not the wife depart from her husband: But and if she depart, let her remain unmarried, or be reconciled to her husband: and let not the husband put away his wife."

I have heard Pastors teach their congregations that in these verses the words wife and husband are really interchangeable. But they are not. The Lord *specifically* commands that the wife not depart from her husband. If the wife departs from her husband she must remain unmarried or go back and be reconciled. God has very serious reasons for this. The verses in Romans 7:1-4 explains this. She is "Bound by the law to her husband as long as he lives." The Lord Commands that the wife should remain unmarried. Why is this? It is because another marriage will interfere with this *being bound*. And it will also dishonor her head (husband or her covering) along with putting herself in greater danger from the Angels. (1 Corinthians 11:1-10) This teaching of remaining unmarried is ignored for the most part because congregations do not spiritually understand what is at stake here.

1 Corinthians 7:12-16 "But to the rest speak I, not the Lord: If any brother hath a wife that believeth not, and she be pleased to dwell with him, let him not put her away. And the woman which hath an husband that believeth not, and if he be pleased to dwell with her, let her not leave him. For the unbelieving husband is sanctified by the wife, and the unbelieving wife is sanctified by the husband: else were your children unclean; but now are they holy. But if the unbelieving depart, let him depart. A brother or a sister is not under bondage in such cases: but God hath called us to peace. For what knowest thou, O wife, whether thou shalt save thy husband? or how knowest thou, O man, whether thou shalt save thy wife?"

Pleased #4909 to think well of in common, i.e. assent to, feel gratified with

Sanctified #37 to make holy; purify, consecrate; (mentally) to venerate [from 40 sacred]

Bondage #1402 to enslave (lit. or fig.) [from 1401 a slave; sense of subjection]

Save #4982 to save; i.e. deliver or protect (lit. or fig.)

Peace #1515 from a primary verb (to join) Peace (lit. or fig.) by implication Prosperity

God's focus on these verses is that He can utilize the marriage institution to bring unbelievers to Himself. Note that even if unbelievers are part of the marriage, the rules assigned to men "Let him not put her away" and for women "Let her not leave him" still apply and are to be obeyed. This is because the man is the *spiritual head* of the woman.

We also read in these verses that God has called us to peace. We are to adjoin and encourage others to unite with Christ. For our spouses, we are used by God to sanctify them. By our sacrifice to God, the power of the Holy Spirit works in our life and is on display to them. This exposes them to God. They may in turn ask for His mercy upon them. In this way can a spouse (save or deliver) their husband or wife. A long time ago in a different mind set, people used to believe that it was God who put marriages together.

Mark 10:9 "What therefore God hath joined together, let not man put asunder."

When a marriage stayed together, God could work in it (both in the good times and bad) to draw a spouse to Him. The child of God witnessed to their spouse by simply obeying Him. Then the marriage could be used to build up the Kingdom of God. Satan hates this. He wants to destroy these marriages. And he can do this through our sexual desires.

1 Corinthians 7:17 "But as God hath distributed to every man, as the Lord hath called every one, so let him walk. And so ordain I in all churches."

God places people in many different situations during their life. Sometimes a mixed in belief couple is what God allows. For His reasons, some of these will be used to bring their spouse and children to Himself. Therefore we should not judge other relationships because it may be that God is working His Will on them. "So let him walk" God tells us. Note: If you are currently in one of these relationships, heed to what God is teaching in these Corinthians verses (what He allows and does not allow). Obey these commands and be used of God for your family. This way, we can serve Heaven and not the world.

In 1 Corinthians 7:18-24, God teaches that we are to serve God and not men. The outward appearance of circumcision means nothing (this serves men). The inward appearance of circumcision (keeping the commandments of God) means everything. Note that the focus is on the manservant in these verses. Should we to apply circumcision to the women in this case? Teachers need to be more discerning about the use of this word. There is a spiritual reason that this involves the male (and not the female) reproductive organ.

1 Corinthians 7:25-28 "Now concerning virgins I have no commandment of the Lord: yet I give my judgment, as one that hath obtained mercy of the Lord to be faithful. I suppose therefore that this is good for the present distress, I say, that it is good for a man so to be. Art thou bound unto a wife? seek not to be loosed. Art thou loosed from a wife? seek not a wife. But and if thou marry, thou hast not sinned; and if a virgin marry, she hath not sinned.

Nevertheless such shall have trouble in the flesh: but I spare you."

Virgin(s) #3933 a maiden; by implication an unmarried daughter

Here, Paul's focus is on the Gospel. This church wanted to know if they should marry off their daughters. Remember, sexual fornication was plaguing this congregation. They wanted to know what direction they should take. Because Paul accepts his present distress or his present constraints on his life, his advice to the congregation was to stay the course. He knew that marriages bring trouble in the flesh. And because Paul is spiritually minded and his teaching was to always obey God, the *trouble in the flesh* he mentions here represent the distractions it will bring between you and your walk with Him. It is better to stay in your present situation.

1 Corinthians 7:29-31 "But this I say, brethren, the time is short: it remaineth, that both they that have wives be as though they had none; And they that weep, as though they wept not; and they that rejoice, as though they rejoiced not; and they that buy, as though they possessed not; And they that use this world, as not abusing it: for the fashion of this world passeth away."

Fashion #4976 a figure (as a mode or circumstance); (by implication) external condition

"For the fashion of this world passeth away." Someone very smart once stated, "All is Vanity." Paul knows that this world's reality, with all of its distractions and enticements becomes so real to a person that the reality of God and of Heaven becomes just a concept in their mind and heart. It is the race or walk that a person does in this world that is of importance. Your focus should not be on your possessions, or what brings you joy or what grieves you in this world. Your focus has to be on Christ. Why? Because the time is short! But Paul also says here that husbands should be as though they had no wife. Why would God allow these words to be said about the marriage?

1 Corinthians 7:32-33 "But I would have you without carefulness. He that is unmarried careth for the things that belong to the Lord, how he may please the Lord: But he that is married careth for the things that are of the world, how he may please his wife."

Carefulness #275 not anxious [from (negative) 1 first & 3308 solicitude]

Careth #3309 to be anxious about [from 3308 solicitude (thru the idea of distraction)]

Paul knew the human condition very well. He understood how weak we are as a whole. We are easily distracted from what really is important. We elevate unimportant matters to the top of our concern list and dwell on them. We worry about the thoughts of others as if they could pass a life or death sentence on us. And we quickly judge the actions of others, many times to distract ourselves from our own actions that desperately need self-examination. What Paul is saying here is that because *our* time is short, those men who have wives should spiritually create a mindset of being unmarried. Their focus needs to be on Christ and serving Him. If a man is married, his heart and mind becomes focused on the world and how to please his wife.

"He that is unmarried careth for the things that belong to the Lord"

This verse seems so out of place in today's society. Is this the mental state of today's men? Unfortunately, the mindset between men and women today is almost the same. We all tend to care for the things that are of this world. We want to please ourselves instead of pleasing the Lord. Paul makes a bold statement here. Is he wrong on this? No. First of all Paul is addressing the *brethren*. Single Christians do care for the things that belong to God. At least the real Christians do. We must understand, the Christianity of today reflects the years of damage done by Satan and his sown tares. Many Biblical instructions are now ignored or excused by many of the churches or denominations, hiding the seriousness of Scripture. Note that a marriage will change how a man pleases from his Lord to his wife. Don't miss this important fact.

1 Corinthians 7:34-35 "There is difference also between a wife and a virgin. The unmarried woman careth for the things of the Lord, that she may be holy both in body and in spirit: but she that is married careth for the things of the world, how she may please her husband. And this I speak for your own profit; not that I may cast a snare upon you, but for that which is comely, and that ye may attend upon the Lord without distraction."

Comely #2158 Well-formed; decorous; noble (in rank) [from 2095 Well and 4976 a figure (as a mode or circumstance)]

Again, (real) single Christian women do care for the things of the Lord, a real desire to be holy in both body and in spirit. In the past people seemed to be aware of God's presence in this world (and in their lives) a lot more then it is today. The *knowing* of God and Heaven were handed down. When I look at many of the congregations today, almost all of the unmarried women (virgins) I see there are more concerned about today's fashion, its trends (fads), or anything else this world produces, than trying to be Holy in body and in Spirit for the Lord. I suspect that most Scriptural passages dealing with behavior have been forgotten or not taught there. Like what we find in the Book of Titus.

Titus 2:3-5 "The aged women likewise, that they be in behaviour as becometh holiness, not false accusers, not given to much wine, teachers of good things; That they may teach the young women to be sober, to love their husbands, to love their children, To be discreet, chaste, keepers at home, good, obedient to their own husbands, that the word of God be not blasphemed."

Titus teaches us a system approved by God to help the next generation of women with their relationship to God. This does not exist in almost all the churches (nor in families for that matter.) Not the way it is taught here nor with the seriousness of eternity at stake. Does anybody really understand what these verses teach us and then apply them? I say again, does anybody really care about these verses? This is a great warning to all of us. And this was a great warning to this church as well. Paul was concerned with all of the distractions that this church was playing around with. He wanted them to worship God correctly and in truth. Worship without distractions.

"There is difference also between a wife and a virgin..."

Do not miss the fact that God points out that there is a spiritual difference between a wife and a virgin. Marriage has a spiritual effect on the woman. She is under the spiritual leadership of her husband. Her *desire* is to him. He is to *rule* over her. This was ordained and applied to mankind by God in the garden of Eden.

1 Corinthians 7:36-38 "But if any man think that he behaveth himself uncomely toward his virgin, if she pass the flower of her age, and need so require, let him do what he will, he sinneth not: let them marry. Nevertheless he that standeth stedfast in his heart, having no necessity, but hath power over his own will, and hath so decreed in his heart that he will keep his virgin, doeth well. So then he that giveth her in marriage doeth well; but he that giveth her not in marriage doeth better."

It is not a sin to marry. God intends people to do this. Desires that we have at times direct our paths. God allows for this. Nevertheless those who both in their heart (standeth stedfast) and in the mind (hath power over his own will) that give up these desires to the Lord are preferred. Our desires are directly connected to our walk with God. That is why He provides us with all of these instructions. Every situation relevant to our relationship to God involves our desires. We must talk to God about our desires and not ignore them.

1 Corinthians 7:39-40 "The wife is bound by the law as long as her husband liveth; but if her husband be dead, she is at liberty to be married to whom she will; only in the Lord. But she is happier if she so

abide, after my judgment: and I think also that I have the Spirit of God."

Bound #1210 a primary verb; to bind (in various applications, literally or figuratively)

Liberty #1658 unrestrained (to go at pleasure), i.e. (as a citizen) not a slave (whether freeborn or manumitted), or (generally) exempt (from obligation or liability) [probably from the article of 2064 to come or go]

Paul will close this chapter by repeating a foundational truth from God. The wife is bound by the law as long as her husband liveth. Bound as long as her husband *lives.* The life or death of the husband determines the spiritual freedom (liberty) of the wife. Again, the Spiritual headship is applied here. Satan had attacked this church through the congregations' sexual desires. The temptations of the physical flesh distracted some members, distorting their understanding of the Will of God. This in turn affected the congregation as they tried to cope with this. Divisions grew and the church begun to splinter into groups that took sides against each other. Some groups became so holy or puffed up, they tolerated some of these acts of the flesh. The Will of God and the truth of it were leaving this church. In this chapter, Paul reminds this congregation of the roles given to the man and the woman. God set up the spiritual order for important reasons. This will accomplish His Will for us on earth.

1 Corinthians 7:1 "Now concerning the things whereof ye wrote unto me: It is good for a man not to touch a woman."

The best way for a man to walk with God would be for him to not touch a woman, be not married, act like you have no wife even though you do, be unmarried so you care more about the Lord, and have power over your own will for this. Why would God teach this? God wants us to attend upon Him without distraction (verse 35). Verse 32 tells us "He that is unmarried careth for the things that belong to the Lord, how he may please the Lord." The man's duty of working for his *Spiritual Bread* is much easier without distractions. The woman is reminded that she is not to depart from her husband and that more importantly; "She is bound by the law to her husband as long as he lives." Some of those in this church were having problems understanding God's Will for the marriage. There is a reason and there is an order for the husband and the wife. Paul reminds them in this chapter. He will also remind those in the Churches at Rome and in Ephesus.

The Covering Of A Woman

In the church of Corinth, contentions in that congregation had divided its members into separate groups. (1:10-11) This was causing the focus to be on others instead of Christ Jesus. (1:12-13) Paul wrote this Epistle to direct them back to the central focus of the Gospel and to bring together these divisions that were separating them. One of these divisions involved the spiritual authority when the men and the women gathered together in the church. In 1 Corinthians 11:1-16, Paul addresses this spiritual headship. We read in verse 3 that this authority is given to the men.

1 Corinthians 11:3 "But I would have you know, that the head of every man is Christ; and the head of the woman is the man; and the head of Christ is God."

Here the word *head* is not talking about a literal head but is used here to describe the pecking order of spiritual authority. The head is the portion of the body that sets the spiritual direction. We read that the head of *every* Man is Christ. And the head of the woman is the man. This is a foundational Truth that started at the Genesis creation. Paul introduces this spiritual headship in verse 3 so when we come to verse 10, we may understand what that passage is teaching.

1 Corinthians 11:4-6 "Every man praying or prophesying, having head covered, dishonoureth his head. But every woman that prayeth or prophesieth with head uncovered dishonoureth her head: for that is even all one as if she were shaven. For if the woman be not covered, let her also be shorn: but if it be a shame for a woman to be shorn or shaven, let her be covered."

Now we are directed toward praying and prophesying, keeping the focus on the spiritual authority. A man is not supposed to have his head covered (it brings dishonour or shame) and a woman is not supposed to have her head uncovered (this brings shame). What is this covering? Is this a literal covering of the head or is it illustrating a spiritual aspect? If the head of the man is Christ, and the head of the woman is the man, then the shame that is brought upon is directed toward Christ and the man. In other words, every man praying or prophesying, having head (or Christ) covered, dishonoureth his head (who is Christ). And every woman that prayeth or prophesieth with head uncovered (no man), dishonoureth her head (who is the man). The covering (or uncovering) is describing a spiritual relationship or way of worshipping. If a man prays with *head covered* he is praying like a woman. And if a woman prays with *head uncovered* she is praying like a man. This was describing what was happening in this Church. (This type of spiritual worship will also be present in the last days.) A woman guilty of praying without a covering was to be shorn as a sign of that act. Once again we see that a literal visible punishment placed on the woman is an outward sign to all of her spiritual rebellion. Note that there is no outward sign for the man given here.

1 Corinthians 11:7 "For a man indeed ought not to cover his head, forasmuch as he is the image and glory of God: but the woman is the glory of the man."

Image #1504 a likeness, i.e. (lit) statute, profile, or (fig) representation, resemblance [from 1503 a primary verb; to resemble]

Glory #1391 Glory (as very apparent), in a wide application (lit or fig, obj or subj) [from the base of 1380 primary verb to think, by impl. to seem (truthfully or uncertainly)]

God now tells us why the man should not pray with his head covered (or to pray like a woman prays). He is the image and glory of God. And because he is made in the image and glory of God, he is the *head* of the woman. He is required to bridge the gap so to speak between the LORD and the woman as her covering. And as he provides this covering for the woman, it should result in *glory* for the man. The woman should reflect the husband's spiritual *walk* with God. In other words, when a man spiritually rules his household according to Scripture, the wife should be a testament (a sign to others) to his obedience to God. She then is the *glory* of the man. Equally important in these verses is that God does not apply the terms image and glory to the woman. God is teaching us in these verses that "the woman is the glory of the man" and that she is *not* the glory of God. So the image and glory are much different for the man and the woman. This is because of how the man and the woman were originally created and the subsequent curse that was applied.

1 Corinthians 11:8-9 *"For the man is not of the woman; but the woman of the man. Neither was the man created for the woman; but the woman for the man."*

In these verses, God reminds us that it is the woman who is the help meet (or an aid) to the man. This requires a subservient position for the woman. Today's couples will be mocked for having this kind of relationship. We have left behind God's blueprint for the man and woman long ago. Even here, Paul reminds this church of basic spiritual order or authority. Man is not of the woman and was not created for the woman. In fact it is exactly the opposite. The spiritual roles that were given to mankind by God were always to be followed. But in today's society, the world tells us that it is the woman who is the spiritual *head* of the house. She is the one who has the compassion, and the wisdom, and the love to direct mankind toward a more civilized society. This Corinthians verse seems so out of place today because we are programmed to believe the exact opposite. It states that the woman was created *for the man* and not the other way around. Note that these verses are still referencing the spiritual headship introduced in verse 3. The church in Corinth was ignoring this basic foundation of truth. Paul had to remind them of this. There is a very important reason that God set up this spiritual authority.

1 Corinthians 11:10 *"For this cause ought the woman to have power on her head because of the angels."*

This verse in Corinthians explains to us why God stresses the spiritual authority given to man. It is because of the angels. What are these angels? And what is this power on her?

Angels #32 to bring tidings; a messenger; by implication a pastor [from 71 to lead, by implication to bring, drive, go, pass or induce]

Power #1849 Privilege, i.e. (subj.) force, capacity, competency, freedom, or (objectively) mastery (concrete magistrate, superhuman, potentate, token of control), delegated influence [from 1832 (in the sense of ability)]

I believe that angels in this context are really *messengers* or what we call Pastors/Priests. (Although this does not rule out an evil spirit or demon.) All throughout mankind's history, we have had these angels (or messengers) preach to the local congregations. Because mankind is not just a flesh creation but also a spiritual being, we can *spiritually connect* with these messengers. There is a huge possibility of being lead down the wrong spiritual path if we are unsure of what is being preached. It was for this reason that man was given the ability and responsibility to spiritually *watch* over the woman. Again, the curse placed on Eve in the Garden is directly responsible for this situation. God made sure that the *power* needed for the woman was provided because it was He that limited her in Genesis 3:16 (by directing her desire and stating that the husband would rule over her). This spiritual application is supported by additional Scripture verses that comment on the woman's spiritual state.

2 Corinthians 11:3 "But I fear, lest by any means, as the serpent beguiled Eve through his subtilty, so your minds should be corrupted from the simplicity that is in Christ."

1 Corinthians 14:34-35 "Let you women keep silence in the churches, it is not permitted unto them to speak, if they learn any thing, let them ask their husbands at home: for it is a shame for women to speak in the church."

1 Timothy 2:11-14 "Let the woman learn in silence, I suffer not a woman to teach, nor usurp authority over the man, but to be in silence, Adam was not deceived, but the woman was in the transgression."

1 Peter 3:7 "Likewise, ye husbands, dwell with them according to knowledge, giving honour unto the wife, as unto the weaker vessel, and as being heirs together of the grace of life; that your prayers be not hindered."

Because the female is the spiritual weaker vessel she is very susceptible or can be easily influenced by these *angels* that bring wrong teachings into the Congregation. Women must rely on someone whose headship is Christ. If a messenger (or angel) delivers a sermon that may be false, God tells us that she must run it by her spiritual authority (or husband) to find out what is correct. For those women who are unmarried, they are given this *covering* from their father. A widow can have a covering from her family or she can place herself under God's covering (by a vow).

1 Corinthians 11:11-12 "Nevertheless neither is the man without the woman, neither the woman without the man, in the Lord. For as the woman is of the man, even so is the man also by the woman; but all things of God."

The curse in Eden was not just for Eve, but for Adam as well. Positions are given and so are responsibilities. We are spiritually intertwined together (in the Lord). The woman is of the man (rib) and the man is by the woman (birth), and all of this by and for God.

1 Corinthians 11:13-15 "Judge in yourselves: is it comely that a woman pray unto God uncovered? Doth not even nature itself teach you, that, if a man have long hair, it is a shame unto him? But if a woman have long hair, it is a glory to her: for her hair is given her for a covering."

In verses 13-15, God continues to teach this spiritual authority and introduces the word hair. Verse 13 does not teach that a woman has to run and get a hat, or a shawl, or a wig if she wants to pray. What this means is that the woman must have some kind of spiritual cover (or authority) over her. Note: we read here that if the woman has long hair, it is a glory to her. Physically this is an outward sign to others. "Is it comely that a woman pray to God uncovered" in these verses still show us that we are talking about spiritual communication.

In this case, her covering is for her spiritual protection. In verse 14, we also read about the long hair that results in shame for the man. We are told that a man is not to have his head covered (verse 4) when praying or prophesying. If a man *covers* his head with a woman's authority, this brings shame. Because God set up the spiritual authority, and this was well understood during the Old and New Testaments, "Doth not even nature itself teach you?"

God teaches the state of men in the Bible who insist upon covering themselves. We read:

Psalm 109:29 "Let mine adversaries be clothed with shame, and let them cover themselves with their own confusion, as with a mantle."

Isaiah 30:1 "Woe to the rebellious children, saith the LORD, that take counsel, but not of me; and that cover with a covering, but not of my spirit, that they may add sin to sin:"

Revelation 9:8 "And they had hair as the hair of women, and their teeth were as of lions."

Here God teaches that those who are false prophets, pastors, and teachers will *spiritually* have their head covered. They will preach to women who pray uncovered and lead them.

Silence In The Church

1 Corinthians 12:1 "Now concerning spiritual gifts, brethren, I would not have you ignorant."

Brethren #80 a Brother (lit. or fig.) [from 1 first (as connective) & the word womb]

In his first letter to the Church at Corinth, Paul brought the congregation into reminisce of some basic rules of the marriage state. He taught how the man and the woman were to handle their sexual urges. Issues of fornication, virgins, and departing from one another were also addressed. (Chapter 7) He goes on to explain who has the spiritual authority in the marriage between the husband and the wife. The headship of this union is given to the man so he may be a *covering* for the woman. (Chapter 11) In Chapter 14, Paul brings this spiritual understanding into the worship service, and reminds them the proper way for men and women to worship together. This congregation had a great zeal to use the spiritual gifts of the Holy Spirit in their fellowship.

1 Corinthians 14:12 "Even so ye, forasmuch as ye are zealous of spiritual gifts, seek that ye may excel to the edifying of the church."

Paul addresses the speaking of tongues during the service and the worth of it, teaching them that this must be done in a proper order if it is to have any edification in the church. Remember, this congregation had many divisions that were disrupting their task to spread the Gospel message. (1 Corinthians 1:11-13) Each division wanted to be the *correct one.*

1 Corinthians 14:26-33 "How is it then, brethren? when ye come together, every one of you hath a psalm, hath a doctrine, hath a tongue, hath a revelation, hath an interpretation. Let all things be done unto edifying. If any man speak in an unknown tongue, let it be by two, or at the most by three, and that by course; and let one interpret. But if there be no interpreter, let him keep silence in the church; and let him speak to himself, and to God. Let the prophets speak two or three, and let the other judge. If any thing be revealed to another that sitteth by, let the first hold his peace. For ye may all prophesy one by one, that all may learn, and all may be comforted. And the spirits of the prophets are subject to the prophets. For God is not the author of confusion, but of peace, as in all churches of the saints."

Brethren #80 a Brother (lit. or fig.) [from 1 first (as connective) & the word womb]

Himself #1438 (from a reflexive pronoun) Him-self

Prophets #4396 a Foreteller (prophet); by analogy an inspired speaker; by extension a poet [from a compound of 4253 "fore", in front of, prior, (fig) superior & 5346 to show or make known one's thoughts, i.e. speak or say]

This may shock some readers but Paul is addressing the men of the congregation here. He is speaking to male *brothers*, to other *men*. Because of what we read in verse 34, that women are to be silent in the church, all those speaking in these verses apply to the men of this congregation. Himself refers to a male. These prophets that speak by two or three are men. How could a woman prophesy in the church if they are to remain silent? They cannot. The spiritual headship given of God must be followed. This congregation had thrown this headship out the window and was operating without it. What is transpiring in this gathering is direct communication between God and the males of this congregation. This is the *natural* spiritual use of the male. The man was given a spiritual responsibility from God to watch over his family. So Paul lays down some basic rules for the men to follow in the worship service. And because they are in a church, Paul reminds them of the law concerning the behavior of the women.

1 Corinthians 14:34 "Let your women keep silence in the churches: for it is not permitted unto them to speak; but they are commanded to be under obedience, as also saith the law."

Women #1135 a woman; spec. a wife [prob. from the base of 1096 cause to be, become]

Silence #4601 to keep silent [from 4602 silence]

Churches #1577 (same # used for Acts & Rev. 2 and 3) a calling out, i.e. (concretely) a popular meeting, especially a religious congregation (Jewish synagogue, or Christian community of members on earth or saints in heaven or both [from a compound of 1537 origin, from, out (of place, time, or cause) & a derivative of 2564 to "call"]

Speak #2980 prolonged form of an otherwise obsolete verb; to talk, i.e. utter words

Obedience #5293 to subordinate; reflexively to obey [from 5259 under & 5021 to arrange in an orderly manner, i.e. assign or dispose]

Pastors' sermons on these verses tend to border on the blasphemous. I've watched as they look across their congregations (mostly women) and try to walk on eggshells when making their comments. When we look at the definitions of the words used here, it is very clear that they mean what they say. Why do you think God wants women to be silent in these worship gatherings? Why are they not permitted to speak? Please note that this is written here with great authority. They are commanded. Why?

"...as also saith the law."

Law #3551 law (through the idea of prescriptive usage), generally (regulation), spec. (of Moses [including the volume]; also of the Gospel) or fig. (a principle)

This is not just an Old Testament law that can be ignored today. God states that this Law is valid for the New Testament era. "Let your women keep silence in the churches." Once again, the curse to womankind in the Garden of Eden directly affects this church, as it affects every church gathering. When these women spoke up in this church, they were *breaking* the Law. Like Miriam in the Old Testament, they wanted to be a prophet and lead. God punished Miriam with leprosy. Here Paul reminds the congregation by simply spelling it out to them. Keep silent. Do not speak.

1 Corinthians 14:35 "And if they will learn any thing, let them ask their husbands at home: for it is a shame for women to speak in the church."

Learn #3129 to learn (in any way)

Shame #149 a shameful thing, i.e. indecorum [neuter (gender) of 150 shameful, i.e. base]

1 Timothy 2:11-12 "Let the woman learn in silence with all subjection. But I suffer not a woman to teach, nor to usurp authority over the man, but to be in silence."

Silence #2271 (as noun) stillness, i.e. desistance from bustle or language [feminine of 2272 keeping one's seat (sedentary), i.e. (by impl.) still (undisturbed, undisturbing)]

The 1 Timothy verses back up what is written here in 1 Corinthians 14. Depend on your husband for information regarding *spiritual things*. And men, how can you answer your wife when you do not know the answer? Men are to study the Word so they can fulfill this command from God. Note that once again (in verse 35) God repeats the main point, woman, do not speak in the church! It is a shame for a woman to do so!

1 Corinthians 14:36 "What? came the word of God out from you? or came it unto you only?"

God answers the critics of this teaching right here. He tells us that the Word of God comes to us (from Him) and not out of us or only to us. Therefore, because God wants a 'men only' discussion, teaching, prophesying gathering, it must be that way. After all, we want to please Him and not ourselves. We are there to worship Him. And we must worship God according to how He commands us.

1 Corinthians 14:37-40 "If any man think himself to be a prophet, or spiritual, let him acknowledge that the

things that I write unto you are the commandments of the Lord. But if any man be ignorant, let him be ignorant. Wherefore, brethren, covet to prophesy, and forbid not to speak with tongues. Let all things be done decently and in order."

Ignorant #50 not to know (lack of info); by implication to ignore (through disinclination)

These are commandments of the Lord. They are to be followed exactly as God teaches us. If a man thinks himself to be a prophet or spiritual, they must acknowledge that what is written here is truth. This by the way, is the man's spiritual responsibility. They should "get wisdom." And with it, "get understanding." This includes learning what is said here about the women. They are to be silent in the churches. Let all things be done decently and in order.

The Husband Is The Head Of The Wife

••••••••••••••••••••••••••••••••

In the book of Ephesians, Paul addresses the conduct of this congregation; bringing to remembrance that not long ago they "walked according to the course of this world." He reminds these *saints* that that they were chosen in Him before the foundation of the world, and that they were predestinated to receive an inheritance. They are not to walk as the Gentiles do in the vanity of their mind, and to grieve not the Holy Spirit that indwells. Instead they are to understand what the Will of the Lord is for each and every one of them.

As with his letters to the other New Testament churches, Paul revisits the spiritual roles given to the man and the woman, and how each one should put into practice the role of submission in the marriage, as this spiritual headship relates as a picture of Christ and the church.

Ephesians 5:21 "Submitting yourselves one to another in the fear of God."

From the Greek we get the word 'Hupotasso' which is a demand to subordinate or obey. In Ephesians, this is the Greek word we are dealing with in this verse.

Submit #5293 to subordinate, reflexively to obey [from 5259 under of place & 5021 a prolonged form of a primary verb-to arrange in an orderly manner, i.e. assign or dispose (to a certain position or lot)]

Submitting #5293 (See above)

Subject #5293 (See above)

Anything done in this "fear of God" will be accomplished according to His Will. What this means is that we subordinate to God first because we fear or reverence Him (and know what the Will of the Lord is), then *out of or from that* we are to submit one to another. This doesn't mean that we immediately submit (reflexively obey) to everybody out of this fear of God. That is not what this verse is teaching. When we are in this "fear of God" we are spiritually ready to help our fellow men, ready to serve where He needs us. So ready are we, that it is an automatic reaction. Now God directs this church (and us) to the inner workings of a marriage. How we are to spiritually submit in the marriage.

Ephesians 5:22 "Wives yourselves unto your own husbands, as unto the Lord."

For many, these verses in Ephesians (22-33) are taught to be only symbolic lessons for us today. After all, the *culture* of that day oppressed their women. Today, we are a more *enlightened* society. Submitting to a husband is something that happens in third world countries or in other religions. Pastors tend to teach that these verses are merely physical or moral. (The man loves & protects the woman & the woman submits & stays with the man.) So these verses are understood in a very superficial way. The teaching about God's spiritual authority for a marriage is completely missing here.

This church was in rebellion against the spiritual curses given out in Eden. Remember, Eve (representing womankind) was cursed with a headship. Her desire is to her husband (diverting her desire to rule as Eve tried to do), and her husband is placed as ruler over her. This is a spiritual rule first and foremost. God will address the husband (or Man's) curse and responsibilities in Ephesians verses 25-29.

The wife submits to her husband as they would submit to the Lord. Do we really understand this today? No. How can a 'wife' go to *Almighty God* and willfully demand a divorce from Him? Today our society (with its secular beliefs and worldly behavior) exemplifies a life far away from what God commands (in the self, in a marriage, and in a congregation). There is no 'fear of God' anymore. So why would our Creator tell the women to treat their husbands as unto the Lord?

Ephesians 5:23 "For the husband is the head of the wife, even as Christ is the head of the church: and he is the saviour of the body."

Head #2776 the head (as the part most readily taken hold of) Literal or Figurative

Wife #1135 woman; specifically a wife [from base of 1096 cause to be; to become]

Church #1577 A calling out, i.e. a popular meeting, religious congregation, Saints in Heaven and/or Earth [from a compound of 1537 origin; out of, from & a derivative of 2564 to call]

Saviour #4990 a Deliverer, i.e. God or Christ [from 4982 to save, deliver, protect]

Body #4983 the body (as a sound whole) lit. or fig.[from 4982 to save, deliver, protect]

The language in this verse sounds similar to what is written to the Church in Corinth.

1 Corinthians 11:3 "But I would have you know, that the head of every man is Christ; and the head of the woman is the man; and the head of Christ is God."

The husband is the head of the wife (the head of the woman is the man). In 1 Corinthians 11, God is teaching His spiritual authority to that church. He does the same with this church in Ephesus. The basic foundation of a spiritual headship has come under attack in every church and congregation throughout mankind's history by Satan. This spiritual authority is meant to point the church in the direction it is to advance and to help keep the congregation in obedience for everyday matters. God wants us to understand that as Christ is the head of the church and is the Saviour of that body, the marriage between a man and a woman must reflect this. That means that the church must be taught and cared for by a Priest of God. In this manner can a husband be the *saviour* of the body (wife).

Isaiah 43:11 "I, even I, am the LORD; and beside me no saviour."

The LORD reminds us in the Book of Isaiah that He's the one and only Saviour.

Ephesians 5:24 "Therefore as the church is subject unto Christ, so let the wives be to their own husbands in every thing."

Every thing #3956 all, any, every, the whole

The church is subject unto Christ, (we know that whatsoever Christ tells the church, the church must follow or it is in rebellion against Him), so then the wives to there own husbands in *every thing*. If God uses the word everything, it means everything. This everything has to be spiritual in nature. And this everything includes the *Word*.

Ephesians 5:25-27 "Husbands, love your wives, even as Christ also loved the church, and gave himself for it. That he might sanctify and cleanse it with the washing of water by the word, That he might present it to himself a glorious church, not having spot, or wrinkle, or any such thing; but that it should be holy and without blemish."

Compare this to what we read in the Book of Ezekiel where God reminds Jerusalem that it was He that brought her to her *glory*.

Ezekiel 16:8-9 "Now when I passed by thee, and looked upon thee, behold, thy time was the time of love; and I spread my skirt over thee, and covered thy nakedness: yea, I sware unto thee, and entered into a covenant with thee, saith the Lord GOD, and thou becamest mine. Then washed I thee with water; yea, I throughly washed away thy blood from thee, and I anointed thee with oil."

Paul is a good example of what the Lord is instructing all of the husbands to do here.

2 Corinthians 11:2 "For I am jealous over you with godly jealousy: for I have espoused you to one

husband, that I may present you as a chaste virgin to Christ."

God reminds the men of the curse given to them in Eden. The husbands are instructed to get in that Word/Scripture garden. A garden cursed with thorns and thistles to hide God's truth. Only through sweat or tribulation is the Word (or the bread of life) understood now. In this passage, God's instructions to the husband mimic instructions for a Priest. The husband is told to love his wife as Christ loved the church and to give his life for it. He is illustrating the husband as Christ and the wife as the church. The husband is to give up his life for it (verse 25), that he might sanctify and cleanse it with the washing of the word (verse 26), so "that he might present it to himself a glorious church…that it should be holy and without blemish" (verse 27). *He* in these verses relate to the husband. *It* in these verses relate to the wife. Note again that God's instructions to the husband includes *by the Word.* God expects the Word to be a part of this duty. Compare this to His instructions to the women.

1 Peter 3:1-2 "Likewise, ye wives, be in subjection to your own husbands; that, if any obey not the word, they also may without the word be won by the conversation of the wives; While they behold your chaste conversation coupled with fear."

They also may without the *word* be won. God is teaching the authoritative positions of a husband and wife using the example of how Christ relates to the church. The spiritual duties of the husband are now long forgotten in almost every marriage. Instead, it is the wife that is the family's *high priest* and the husband and kids submit to her. Please understand that Christ gave up his life for the church but he *never* submitted himself to it.

Ephesians 5:28-30 "So ought men to love their wives as their own bodies. He that loveth his wife loveth himself. For no man ever yet hated his own flesh; but nourisheth and cherisheth it, even as the Lord the church. For we are members of his body, of his flesh, and of his bones."

We men must love our wives as our own bodies (as Christ [who is the head] loves His body the church). Christ does not hate his body (the church) but gives it nourishment so it will live. Likewise we men are to nourish our own body (wife) with the Word of God. This is how the body, flesh, and bones are to operate as a unit. (I believe that this is an illustration of Jesus, the man, and the woman.)

Ephesians 5:31-32 "For this cause shall a man leave his father and mother, and shall be joined unto his wife, and they two shall be one flesh. This is a great mystery: but I speak concerning Christ and the church."

"For this cause…" God has very specific reasons for this type of union between the man and woman. It's not just for having children, there is a spiritual headship that is provided. (We have a weaker vessel that must be considered.) A 'head' covering is created because of the *Angels*. The man leaves father and mother and is joined to his wife. Bone (woman) becomes flesh (man) and they are both one. The man is the "saviour of the body." Spiritually, both the man and woman are in submission to the Holy Spirit, each fulfilling the marital roles assigned by God. The great mystery in verse 32 is that this marriage becomes a living example of Jesus Christ and His church. The two become one. In a physical aspect, the two (man flesh and woman flesh) become one (baby flesh).

Ephesians 5:33 "Nevertheless let every one of you in particular so love his wife even as himself; and the wife see that she reverence her husband."

God sums up this chapter by again stressing basic roles for the man and the woman.

Husbands love your wives. God has to tell men to love their wives. If they love their wife, then they can "sanctify and cleanse her with the washing of water by the word."

Wives, reverence your husbands. God has to tell women to reverence their husbands.

Reverence #5399 to frighten, to be alarmed, to be in awe of, revere [from 5401 to be put in fear, alarm, or fright]

God gives the women another clue in how to submit to their husband. Reverence your husband, be in awe of, revere or fear. These are things they should be doing to God, so they can apply this submission accordingly to their husbands.

Note that this positional spiritual teaching continues in Ephesians chapter 6, children to parents, servants to masters, and finally believers to our God. It is because we wrestle not against flesh & blood, but against principalities, against powers, rulers of the darkness of this world, against spiritual wickedness. These are spiritual instructions for us. This is to help us be a faithful (spiritual) ruler over what God gives to each and every one.

Matthew 24:44-47 "Therefore be ye also ready: for in such an hour as ye think not the Son of man cometh. Who then is a faithful and wise servant, whom his lord hath made ruler over his household, to give them meat in due season? Blessed is that servant, whom his lord when he cometh shall find so doing. Verily I say unto you, That he shall make him ruler over all his goods."

Let The Woman Learn In Silence

In the book of 1 Timothy, there are two very important teachings that we must consider when understanding the man and the woman's spiritual positions of authority. The first one is found in chapter 2.

1 Timothy 2:7 "Whereunto I am ordained a preacher, and an apostle, (I speak the truth in Christ, and lie not;) a teacher of the Gentiles in faith and verity."

Ordained #5087 to place (in the widest application, lit. and fig.; properly in a passive or horizontal posture)

Truth #225 truth [from 227 true (as not concealing)]

Paul is an apostle of Jesus Christ. He can speak the truth to us without *lie*. This is because his spirit is under the control of the Holy Spirit. What this means is that we must heed the words that are written down here. These instructions are from God. Paul is merely the messenger. Timothy is instructed in how the church is to conduct itself (both within and without) and how to oversee this. He starts with those who are in charge. As with Paul's other letters to the churches, he addresses the spiritual differences and responsibilities between the man and the woman in this matter. He begins with the men's conduct first.

1 Timothy 2:8 "I will therefore that men pray every where, lifting up holy hands, without wrath and doubting."

The description of how men are to pray is given here. We are to be without wrath and doubting when communicating to God. This reflects a right relationship with our Lord to others. For many this brings about the lifting up of holy hands. From the outside, men are to witness to others in how they conduct themselves daily. What about the women? Do we read about (holy hands) for her? No. We are to focus on the woman's apparel or the ornaments she uses. We are to look at the way they are dressed in and out of the church.

1 Timothy 2:9-10 "In like manner also, that women adorn themselves in modest apparel, with shamefacedness and sobriety; not with broided hair, or gold, or pearls, or costly array; But (which becometh women professing godliness) with good works."

Here God describes the woman's outside apparel. This *apparel* should reflect to others a right relationship to God. This is an interesting comparison, the men with holy hands, and the woman with modest apparel. In the congregation, women are not to compete where the focus is directed during the worship. The spotlight should not be on her. With just her clothing, a woman can *speak* (or express herself) in the church. She is to dress for God, and not for herself. She is to help the church stay focused on the Lord and not draw it away from Him; this is the time to worship God. And this command from Him to the women has its roots in the Old Testament.

1 Peter 3:5 "For after this manner in the old time the holy women also, who trusted in God, adorned themselves, being in subjection unto their own husbands:"

With the outward appearance explained, Paul now directs us to the inward differences between the sexes. He will address the spiritual authority between the man and the woman that was designated to them in the Garden of Eden.

1 Timothy 2:11 "Let the woman learn in silence with all subjection."

Learn #3129 to learn (in any way)

Silence #2271 (as noun) stillness, i.e. desistance from bustle or language [feminine of 2272 properly keeping one's seat (sedentary) i.e. (by implication still]

Subjection #5292 subordination [from 5293 to subordinate, reflexively to obey]

"Let the woman learn in silence with all subjection." She is to be silent in the church. This command from God has been compromised in almost all of today's congregations. From the pulpit you can now hear a woman preach a sermon or teach a Bible study. Many are asked to help lead in some verbal way during a worship service. Pastors have either given in to pressure from the congregation or have been ordered to do this from those who lead their denominations. To counter this, Paul shares some Biblical basics with Timothy regarding the woman's place in the church and in the home.

1 Timothy 2:12 "But I suffer not a woman to teach, nor to usurp authority over the man, but to be in silence."

Suffer #2010 to turn over (transfer) i.e. allow

Teach #1321 a prolonged (causative) form of a primary verb {dao} to learn; to teach (in the same broad application)

Usurp #831 to act of oneself, i.e. (fig) dominate

This is not difficult to understand. The woman is not to teach, nor usurp authority over the man. She is to learn in silence. Remember that Pentecost has already occurred. The pouring out of God's Spirit upon all flesh has happened. It did not change the spiritual authority that God set up in the Garden of Eden. In fact, Paul uses that example to back up why the women should be silent in the church. Why they are not to teach men.

1 Timothy 2:13-14 "For Adam was first formed, then Eve. And Adam was not deceived, but the woman being deceived was in the transgression."

Deceived #538 of uncertain derivation; a cheat, i.e. delude

Transgression #3847 violation [from 3845 to go contrary to, i.e. violate a command]

Adam failed in his job of watching over his (congregation.) So therefore each man is given the responsibility to lead his household. This means one teacher and one authority for each home. This is the direct result of the woman being deceived in the transgression.

1 Timothy 2:15 "Notwithstanding she shall be saved in childbearing, if they continue in faith and charity and holiness with sobriety."

Saved #4982 to save, i.e. deliver or protect (lit. or fig.)

Childbearing #5042 childbirth (parentage), i.e. (by impl.) maternity (the performance of maternal duties) [from the same as 5041 to be a child-bearer, i.e. parent (mother)]

"Notwithstanding she shall be saved in childbearing." Should we take this literally? The woman will only be saved if she gives birth to a child? (And that she continues in faith and charity and holiness with sobriety?) So if they do not bear a child, Salvation is lost to them? Is this what this verse is teaching? The common understanding of this passage is that through a line of *babies* that the women give birth to will eventually produce the Savior Jesus Christ. This will *save* her. But this Old Testament direct line to Jesus Christ does not include all women. And it does not address all of the *babies* that are born of woman after the birth of Jesus. Because she is the matrix for sinners to come into this world, the woman received a special kind of sorrow (childbirth sorrow) that she was to experience in giving birth. This is an exclusive responsibility handed to the women. Men were not cursed with this. And you can easily read in Scripture the importance of women having children. It was a big deal if one was *barren.* (1 Sam 1:5-6) Women claimed they were not *blessed* of God. They would pray and lament to Him for a child. (Gen 30:22-23) Sometimes the punishment the Lord would hand out would include closing up wombs. (Gen 20:18) So if we must take this verse literally it will be a shock to many women. Isn't it interesting that in the times that we live in, the issues of Birth control and Abortion have become the major spiritual stumblingblocks to most women? These stumblingblocks directly oppose what these verses in 1 Timothy teach. So what is the truth? Let us consider what God is teaching in this Luke passage.

Luke 2:23 "(As it is written in the law of the Lord, Every male that openeth the womb shall be called holy to the Lord;)"

Where is this written in the law of the Lord? We find this in the Book of Exodus.

Exodus 13:2 "Sanctify unto me all the firstborn, whatsoever openeth the womb among the children of Israel, both of man and of beast: it is mine."

When a male is born to the world, we have a *head* of a household. This head is responsible for those he *rules*. A woman can marry this man and come under his spiritual authority. It is not just Jesus Christ that 1 Timothy 2:15 is referring to, but to the men "that openeth the womb" and are "called holy to the Lord." In this way, the literal interpretation fits. In addition, the 1 Timothy verses involve a husband. In a marriage the husband and wife are called the *one flesh*. And in this marriage the husband is the spiritual leader of the wife. Because of this he is called to "sanctify and cleanse it with the washing of water by the word." *It* referring to the wife.

Ephesians 5:25-27 "Husbands, love your wives, even as Christ also loved the church, and gave himself for it; That he might sanctify and cleanse it with the washing of water by the word, That he might present it to himself a glorious church, not having spot, or wrinkle, or any such thing; but that it should be holy and without blemish."

We husbands are spiritually responsible for our own *Eve*. For our "weaker vessel."

1 Peter 3:7 "Likewise, ye husbands, dwell with them according to knowledge, giving honour unto the wife, as unto the weaker vessel, and as being heirs together of the grace of life; that your prayers be not hindered."

We are heirs together of the grace of life. This is a big clue. Doesn't this describe our relationship with Jesus? We are His spiritual *brides*. He is our spiritual husband.

Ephesians 5:23 "For the husband is the head of the wife, even as Christ is the head of the church: and he is the saviour of the body."

God has given men this spiritual authority for His purpose. It is an integral part of God's Salvation plan. God is very, very serious about His marriage program.

Ezekiel 16:38 "And I will judge thee, as women that break wedlock and shed blood are judged; and I will give thee blood in fury and jealousy."

We should understand that just because a woman gives birth she is not saved. She is to be married before this birth happens. She is then *one flesh* (which are heirs together of the grace of life) with her husband. She now has a headship. A *saviour* of the body. For more information on this subject see the chapter titled "The husband is the head of the wife."

1 Timothy 2:15 "Notwithstanding she shall be saved in childbearing, if they continue in faith and charity and holiness with sobriety."

Even with the childbearing, they must continue in faith and charity and holiness with sobriety. Believing Faith in Jesus Christ as Lord and Saviour. And behavior of charity and holiness with sobriety. I believe that this is the teaching of this verse.

The next important point is found in chapter 5. This deals with the issue of widowhood.

1 Timothy 5:3-5 "Honour widows that are widows indeed. But if any widow have children or nephews, let them learn first to shew piety at home, and to requite their parents: for that is good and acceptable before God. Now she that is a widow indeed, and desolate, trusteth in God, and continueth in supplications and prayers night and day."

Widows #5503 a widow (as lacking a husband) lit. or fig. [feminine of a presumed derivation apparently from the base of 5490 (a "chasm" or vacancy) through the idea of deficiency]

Requite #287 (to exchange); requital, #591 to give away, i.e. up, over, back, etc. (in various applications) [from 575 "off" i.e. away and 1325 to give (used in a very wide application)]

A widow *indeed* must be desolate, (no family member to care for her) someone who trusts in God, and is continuous in her supplications and prayers night and day. To be a widow indeed is to be honored as a handmaid of God. This woman has the Lord as her spiritual *covering*. This is a classification that needed to be decided by the church. A great example of a widow indeed is found in the book of Luke. She is called Anna, a prophetess.

Luke 2:36-37 "And there was one Anna, a prophetess, the daughter of Phanuel, of the tribe of Aser: she was of a great age, and had lived with an husband *seven years from her virginity; And she was a widow of about fourscore and four years, which departed not from the temple, but served God with fastings <u>and prayers night and day</u>."*

This was a widow's qualification. To serve God and to pray to Him both night and day. Her focus in serving the Lord included no other man in her life. That door was closed. This included a vow to God, and she was strictly held accountable to Him for this vow. Paul now tells Timothy that there should be an age limit for the widows.

1 Timothy 5:9-10 "Let not a widow be taken into the number under threescore years old, having been the wife of one man, Well reported of for good works; if she have brought up children, if she have lodged strangers, if she have washed the saints' feet, if she have relieved the afflicted, if she have diligently followed every good work."

Work(s) #2041 toil (as an effort or occupation); by implication an act.

If the widow was under the age of sixty, Timothy should refuse her request to be a widow. Why? What difference does it make if the woman is less than 60 years old?

1 Timothy 5:11-12 "But the younger widows refuse: for when they have begun to wax wanton against Christ, they will marry; Having damnation, because they have cast off their first faith."

Wax #2691 Wanton #2691 to become voluptuous against [from 2596 down (in place or time) and 4763 to be luxurious]

Damnation #2917 a decision (the function or the effect, for or against "crime") [from 2919 properly to distinguish, i.e. decide (mentally or judicially); by implication to try, condemn, punish]

What a statement Paul makes on these younger widows. When they have begun to wax wanton against Christ, they will marry. This will break their vow to God. This will bring damnation to them (because they have cast off their first faith). Their faith in Christ as their covering. So what happens to the woman who now has damnation from God?

1 Timothy 5:13 "And withal they learn to be idle, wandering about from house to house; and not only idle, but tattlers also and busybodies, speaking things which they ought not."

Tattlers #5397 a garrulous person, i.e. prater.

Busybodies #4021 working all around, i.e. officious (meddlesome, neuter (gender) plural magic) [from 4012 prop. through (all over, i.e. around; fig. with respect to) and 2041 toil (as an effort or occupation); by implication an act]

These women no longer serve our Lord. They serve themselves. They are in a sense, practicing adultery against Christ. They become a force against the family of God. This behavior in verse 13 (idle, tattlers, busybodies, speaking things they should not) sounds like the *ways* of the evil one. This will help destroy those around them. Consider the amount of divorced or widowed women under sixty in today's society. And the great influence they have over their women friends. Many become *support groups* for those who are considering divorce from their husbands, giving them unbiblical advice to follow.

So these widows that are under the age of sixty should marry again and come under the headship of a man. This should produce Godly behavior (if the husband also obeys the headship of Christ upon him.)

1 Timothy 5:14-15 "I will therefore that the younger women marry, bear children, guide the house, give none occasion to the adversary to speak reproachfully. For some are already turned aside after Satan."

Turned #1624 to deflect, i.e. turn away (lit. or fig.) [from 1537 a primary prep. denoting origin (the point whence motion or action proceeds), from, out (of place, time, or cause) and the base of 5157 a turn ("trope"), i.e. revolution (fig. variation)]

Satan #4567 the accuser, i.e. the devil

For some have already turned aside after Satan. From the beginning of this church system we are told here that women already were falling prey to the *roaring lion.* This statement in 1 Timothy exposes the spiritual weakness of the woman. The young widowed woman should marry because they need this headship. They need a spiritual *power* on their head.

1 Corinthians 11:10 "For this cause ought the woman to have power on her head because of the angels."

The Weaker Vessel

1 Peter chapter 2 instructs the Christian of the self-sacrifices that are expected from them. It stresses that submission to authority is doing the Will of God for His servants. We are to offer up spiritual sacrifices to God in verse 5. Abstain from fleshly lusts in verse 11. In verses 13 and 14, we submit to every ordinance of man (the laws of the land). And servants are to be subject to their masters in verse 18 (whether they are good or bad).

1 Peter 2:20 "For what glory is it, if, when ye be buffeted for your faults, ye shall take it patiently? but if, when ye do well, and suffer for it, ye take it patiently, this is acceptable with God."

A certain amount of personal anguish (which we are to do patiently) when done in God's service is acceptable with God. The next verse explains to us why.

1 Peter 2:21 "For even hereunto were ye called: because Christ also suffered for us, leaving us an example, that ye should follow his steps:"

Suffering is in the game plan for a child of God. It is required. We should "follow his steps." Do not revile, do not threaten others as verse 23 teaches. Our Lord tells us that (for even hereunto) we were called. "Take it patiently, this is acceptable with God."

This theme of self-sacrifice and submission to authority continues in Chapter 3.

1 Peter 3:1-7 "Likewise, ye wives, be in subjection to your own husbands; that, if any obey not the word, they also may without the word be won by the conversation of the wives; While they behold your chaste conversation coupled with fear. Whose adorning let it not be that outward adorning of plaiting the hair, and of wearing of gold, or of putting on of apparel; But let it be the hidden man of the heart, in that which is not corruptible, even the ornament of a meek and quiet spirit, which is in the sight of God of great price. For after this manner in the old time the holy women also, who trusted in God, adorned themselves, being in subjection unto their own husbands: Even as Sara obeyed Abraham, calling him lord: whose daughters ye are, as long as ye do well, and are not afraid with any amazement. Likewise, ye husbands, dwell with them according to knowledge, giving honour unto the wife, as unto the weaker vessel, and as being heirs together of the grace of life; that your prayers be not hindered."

The words *likewise* and *subjection* are directed at the wives in verses 1-6.

Note: that likewise (and not subjection) is applied to the husbands in verse 7.

Likewise #3668 Similarly [adverb from 3664 similar (in appearance or character)]

Subjection #5293 to Subordinate; **reflexively to obey**. [from 5259 under & 5021 to arrange in an orderly manner; i.e. to assign or dispose (to a certain position or lot)]

To fully comprehend what is taught here, we need to look at this passage in more detail.

1 Peter 3:1-2 "Likewise, ye wives, be in subjection to your own husbands; that, if any obey not the word, they also may without the word be won by the conversation of the wives; While they behold your chaste conversation coupled with fear."

Chaste #53 properly Clean; (fig) innocent; modest, perfect [from the same as 40 sacred]

Conversation #391 Behavior [from 390 to overturn, also to return; by implication to busy oneself, i.e. remain, live]

Fear #5401 (to be put in fear) alarm; or fright

God is commanding the wives to obey the roles given to them "be in subjection to your own husbands." The wife must have this foundational position if she is to witness to her husband who is not obeying the word. In 1 Peter 2 verses 21-24, Christ shows us how His self-sacrifice and submission to authority resulted in *saving* souls. This example is to be followed. God tells the wives to do likewise if they are to have any success in *winning* their husband back to God. These are the spiritual duties of a help meet.

1 Corinthians 11:3 "But I would have you know, that the head of every man is Christ; and the head of the woman is the man; and the head of Christ is God."

This Spiritual Order from God must be followed even if the husband is not obeying the word. God teaches that it is through this *method*, success (with God's Blessing) may happen. So how does this method work? The husband would watch (or behold) his wife coping with day-to-day problems (internal as well as external) by her obediently waiting on God or showing a spiritual peace in the midst of some turmoil. She is witnessing to her (one flesh) God's Way. This is chaste conversation coupled with fear. This living example (which God is requiring here) can result in the husband being *won*. Today we are so far away from this method; it's a miracle that it is still practiced by some.

Won #2770 to Gain (lit. or fig.) [from 2771 gain]

Word #3056 Something said (including the thought); a Topic (subject or discourse); Reasoning (the mental faculty); Motive; the Divine Expression (Christ) [from 3004 lay forth; relate] [NOTE: IT SAYS WITHOUT THE WORD]

The being *won* here is to come back to the Word. The husband observes his wife behaving like a daughter of God should, and it brings his own thoughts or desires back to the Lord where they should be focused on. God has given women a unique ability (they can witness to their husbands utilizing submission to authority as a tool.)

1 Timothy 2:12 "But I suffer not a woman to teach, nor to usurp authority over the man, but to be in silence."

Because of the curse that was placed upon womankind in the Garden of Eden, women are not to teach or usurp authority over the man. This is a spiritual command from God. And so this is why 1 Peter 3 says "without the word." Compare this to "by the word" as we read in Ephesians chapter 5.

Ephesians 5:25-27 "Husbands, love your wives, even as Christ also loved the church, and gave himself for it; That he might sanctify and cleanse it with the washing of water by the word, That he might present it to himself a glorious church, not having spot, or wrinkle, or any such thing; but that it should be holy and without blemish."

The husband is required to utilize the Word when fulfilling his duties in the marriage. This difference between the sexes is very important. Spiritually, they must follow God's system in order to be *blessed* by Him. They are heirs together of the Grace of Life. This teaching is almost completely ignored by the churches and the local congregations, and so wives spiritually lead in their homes. (And the husband allows this to happen.) These husbands are not *watching* over what God has given them. They are not good stewards of this gift. Their children observe this and are taught by example how to disobey God. Through many generations this understanding of spiritual duties has faded away.

Don't miss the fact that Peter has to remind the "Elect according to the foreknowledge of God the Father" some basic facts. As Paul wrote to each of the churches reminding them of the spiritual authority set down by God, so does Peter remind them in this letter.

1 Peter 3:3-4 "Whose adorning let it not be that outward adorning of plaiting the hair, and of wearing of gold, or of putting on of apparel; But let it be the hidden man of the heart, in that which is not corruptible, even the ornament of a meek and quiet spirit, which is in the sight of God of great price."

Adorning #2889 Orderly arrangement, decoration, the world [from the base of 2865 to provide for; to carry off]

Outward #1855 External [from 1854 out]

Hidden #2927 Concealed, i.e. private [from 2928 to conceal (by covering)]

Ornament (no Strong's # offered)

In these verses, God teaches the ladies what He considers spiritual beauty (a great price). On the one hand we have the outward adorning. Dressing the body with hair, gold, and apparel. This adorning is for the self; it expresses the *self-image.* We can view this as earthly, a demand to be noticed. This is the way of fashion in our society today, it wants the world's attention. And this adulation for the self is in direct conflict with our worship of God. Many women today are in great danger of only focusing on their outside adorning. The husband is to help them in this area. But I find that most men are afraid to spiritually lead their wives.

When a wife is practicing "chaste conversation" in obedience to God (for the benefit of her husband), she is not focusing on decorating her outside. She is directing her focus inward toward her spirit. She desires that her heart be *adorned* with the hidden man. Who is this hidden man? Is this the Holy Spirit in that which is not corruptible? I believe that a woman *wins* her husband by this hidden man of the heart or by the Holy Spirit that dwells within. God can witness through the woman in this way.

"But let it be the hidden man of the heart, in that which is not corruptible."

Man #444 Man-faced, i.e. a human being [from 435 a man & the countenance of 3700 to gaze (i.e. with wide-open eyes, as at something remarkable]

Heart #3820 the heart; also used (fig) very widely for the feelings, the will and even the intellect; likewise for the center of anything [a form of 3824 the heart (as the most interior organ) used also like 3820]

God does not use the appellative hidden woman. He uses the term "hidden man." Why is that? Is this significant? We find that God's spiritual order for mankind is reflected here.

If the woman has a hidden man (man-faced) in her heart, it reflects *outside* to others a right relationship to God. And she is to continue to adorn her heart, resulting in a meek and quiet spirit. Note that in scripture once again, the woman's appearance in public (clothes, jewelry, or her hair) is a sign of her relationship to God. But does the Lord really care how a woman dresses? Yes, it is very important to Him.

Deuteronomy 22:5 "The woman shall not wear that which pertaineth unto a man, neither shall a man put on a woman's garment: for all that do so are abomination unto the LORD thy God."

God has Laws that we don't always understand, but they are important for the plans He has for mankind. Women influence others by the *image* they project. They can entice others just by how they physically present themselves. Here in Deuteronomy a woman dressing as a man goes against the *image* God desires. It is an abomination to Him.

1 Peter 3:5 "For after this manner in the old time the holy women also, who trusted in God, adorned themselves, being in subjection unto their own husbands:"

Holy #40 Sacred (physically pure, morally blameless/religious, ceremonial consecrated)

Trusted # [hoping #1679] to expect or confide [from 1680 expectation; confidence]

Subjection #5393 to Subordinate; **reflexively to obey**. [from 5259 under & 5021 to arrange in an orderly manner; i.e. to assign or dispose (to a certain position or lot)]

Holy women *adorned* themselves in this way. They had a meek and quiet spirit. They had a meek and quiet spirit because they *trusted in God*. Note that being in subjection unto their husbands was a given here. This behavior was expected from them.

1 Peter 3:6 "Even as Sara obeyed Abraham, calling him lord: whose daughters ye are, as long as ye do well, and are not afraid with any amazement."

Obeyed #5219 to hear under (as a subordinate), i.e. to listen attentively; by implication to heed or conform to a command or authority [from 5259 under & 191 to hear]

Lord #2962 Supreme in authority, i.e. (as noun) controller; by implication Mr. (title)

Amazement #4423 alarm [from 4422 (through the idea of causing to fall or through that of causing to fly away) to scare]

God shows us an example of this meek and quiet spirit. Her name is Sara (Sarah), the wife of Abraham. He describes her as holy and one who trusts in God. She obeys what she knows of His Will. We read: "whose daughters ye are, as long as ye do well." Our Lord teaches us that this submission is His ultimate desire for the marriage. Today this behavior of submission to the husband is taught as being destructive for the woman. And this is taught in the world as well as in many churches. This causes many women to be "afraid with amazement." (They fear a belief of the world more than their God.) They do not call their husband *lord.* Sara calls Abraham lord because he is the "saviour of the body" and "the head of the wife" as we read in Ephesians.

Ephesians 5:22-24 "Wives, submit yourselves unto your own husbands, as unto the Lord. For the husband is the head of the wife, even as Christ is the head of the church: and he is the saviour of the body. Therefore as the church is subject unto Christ, so let the wives be to their own husbands in every thing."

Sarah has placed herself under her husband's *headship or covering* because she trusts in God and not in man. She *spiritually* understands where her trust is to be placed.

In Abraham's day, in the time of Jesus, and now today, all women are to do the same.

1 Peter 3:7a "Likewise, ye husbands, dwell with them according to knowledge, giving honour unto the wife, as unto the weaker vessel,"

According #2596 a primary particle: down (in place or time) in varied relations (according to the case with which it is joined)

Knowledge #1108 knowing (the act), i.e. (by implication) knowledge [from 1097 a prolonged form of a primary verb; to know (absolutely) in a great variety of applications]

We husbands are not just to *dwell* but are also to rule over our household (our family).

Luke 12:42-43 "And the Lord said, Who then is that faithful and wise steward, whom his lord shall make ruler over his household, to give them their portion of meat in due season? Blessed is that servant, whom his lord when he cometh shall find so doing."

God stresses two very important points to the husband in 1 Peter 3:7a. First, the men are to dwell with their wives according to *knowledge.* All right, whose knowledge?

If the husband leads his household according to his wife's knowledge, he cannot be the steward God instructs of them in these Luke verses. To desire knowledge of God and His commandments is the duty of every husband. Scripture was always to be studied by the head of the house. This *knowledge* increased for the husband to help him lead his household more obediently to the Word. In addition, the husband was to teach those who were under his care. This ties into our second point, the husband is to give honour to the wife, "as unto the weaker vessel."

Honour #5092 a value, i.e. money paid, or (concretely and collectively) valuables; by analogy esteem or the dignity [from 5099 to pay a price, i.e. as a penalty]

Weaker #772 strengthless (in various applications, literally, figuratively and morally) [from 1 (as a negative particle) the first and the base of 4599 to strengthen, i.e. (fig) conform (in spiritual knowledge and power)]

Vessel #4632 a vessel, implement, equipment or apparatus (literally or figuratively [specifically a wife as contributing to the usefulness of the husband])

So, how does one give "honour unto the wife, as unto the weaker vessel?" How does one (esteem value) to the wife, as the spiritually challenged one? This takes *knowledge.*

We husbands give honor (or esteem) to our wives by patiently dealing with them with love and understanding. We do this because we understand their spiritual position. They need our help because of the spiritual curse placed upon them in the Garden of Eden. And so God tells us that the woman is the weaker vessel. This weakness is in spiritual strength and knowledge.

How can this be? Many church groups teach that spiritually both the man and woman are the same. But here in 1 Peter, God teaches us the exact opposite. Oh I see, they look at this verse and believe that it is physical. The woman is weaker physically. Where did this interpretation (or doctrine) of this physical weakness originate? It came from the mind of men. The focus of these 1 Peter 3 verses is on spiritual things, not earthly. Just look at the rest of this verse:

1 Peter 3:7b "...and as being heirs together of the grace of life; that your prayers be not hindered."

Heirs #4789 a co-heir, i.e. participant in common [from 4862 union and 2818 a sharer by lot, i.e. inheritor]

Grace #5485 graciousness (as gratifying), of manner or act (abstr. or concr., lit. fig., or **spiritual**; especially the divine influence upon the heart, and its reflection in the life)

Life #2222 life (lit or fig) [from 2198 a primary verb: to live (lit or fig)]

Prayers #4335 prayer **(worship)**; by implication an oratory (chapel) [from 4336 to pray to God, i.e. supplicate, worship]

Hindered#1581 to exscind; fig. to frustrate [from 1537 origin (the point whence motion or action proceeds) and 2875 a primary verb; to chop; to beat the breast in grief]

This union between a husband and a wife is much more than just a legal piece of paper. God teaches us that they become one flesh, heirs-together. Therefore, we must pray and worship in a way that is pleasing (and commanded) by God. This *grace* our Lord applies to the hearts of a married couple is His divine influence. A marriage needs this spiritual guidance every day. When we pray correctly to Him, our one flesh or (temple) is not hindered. Our sacrifices that we offer up to God are pleasing to Him.

Ephesians 5:28-29 "So ought men to love their wives as their own bodies. He that loveth his wife loveth himself. For no man ever yet hated his own flesh; but nourisheth and cherisheth it, even as the Lord the church:"

The man is to nourisheth (teach) and cherisheth (honor) it (his one flesh). It is his job.

Today, many think that it is the man who is the weaker vessel (spiritually as well as in other ways). That mindset, presented as reality from nearly everywhere you look, ends up becoming the mindset accepted in many homes of the faithful. Too many men accept this position under their wives as the spiritual leader. She is the one in the home who spiritually directs the family, and so the husband follows the wife's spiritual lead in a submissive way. Unfortunately, this behavior is passed on as acceptable to their children. This kind of *worship* is in direct opposition to the way God created us. We must not forget that we were created to worship God His way.

John 4:24 "God is a Spirit: and they that worship him must worship him in spirit and in truth."

So what should a husband do to please his Lord? What should he do to receive God's daily blessings and guidance for his family? He must take full responsibility for his spiritual position. And he must fulfill what God commands in Scripture all the duties of a spiritual leader. Note that God ties the marriage relationship and its spiritual order to the Grace of Life. Our prayers and requests to Him are affected. And wives, if you challenge your husband's spiritual authority, you are hindering this method we are to follow. Focus on *submitting* to the Lord. When you have done so, submitting to your husband will be natural. You will **(reflexively obey)** the spiritual position that God has given you.

Spiritual Revelation

Spiritual life in the Roman Catholic Church was simple. I was told what to believe and hence, how to worship. As a child I was baptized, received Holy Communion and completed the confirmation sacrament. My understanding of what the Scriptures taught was sparse at best, so I depended completely upon what the church instructed. However, as I began to read the Bible in earnest, some doctrines taught by the church seemed to directly conflict with certain passages; and some of those not just in conflict; but having opposing dogmas. This had me questioning personal beliefs that were my foundation for most of my *religious* life. Meetings with Church elders and Priests as to why there were obvious differences between what the church and Scripture taught were unfruitful. I was told immediately not to question the Catholic doctrines. This was absolute truth from God. This did not sit well with me, and so my search to authenticate the real Gospel from Scripture began. It was shortly afterward I left this institution.

It was during this time that I experienced several (what some would label) *supernatural encounters* that could not be explained from any spiritual knowledge understood by me. I would find out later that these were the dreams and visions promised to us from the Book of Acts. (Acts 2:17) The most noteworthy (and the one that left the most impact upon me) was what I label an out of the body dream. It was different from an ordinary dream because I was totally aware of everything that was happening. This awareness began as I felt a part of me drift above my flesh. Looking down upon my body (that was in a sleeping position), I slowly observed everything in the room. Every detail of each object was crystal clear to me, even in the darkness. There was neither fear nor anxiousness in my being, but a calm acceptance of this experience. Suddenly a feeling of lightness came upon me as I slowly drifted upward toward the ceiling and passing through it. The next thing that came into view was the top of the building, which began to grow smaller and smaller in size as I continued to ascend upward. Soon blocks of houses replaced the one building until they also became too small to see in any detail. It was at this time a light mist began to surround me. I turned my view upward to see that I had entered into a section of light condensation. That was when I noticed that just ahead lay a huge bank of bright white clouds. It shined brilliance unknown to me, and was so thick I could not see through them. I knew this was my destination. Unfortunately my acute awareness left me upon entering into these clouds, for I have no memory of what transpired there but only the feeling of passage of time. I believe that this place represented Heaven, and recollection during my stay there was forbidden. My next cognizant thought was leaving this location and returning to my sleeping body, awakening upon the rejoining of my spirit to my flesh. Sitting up immediately I tried to make sense of this experience. After several minutes it dawned on me that even though the Catholic religion had instructed me about my body and soul, God had just showed me something more, that I had a living spirit.

Intrigued by this spiritual experience, I sought to know more. The established religions I knew offered no further information, so I searched for any books that dealt with this subject. Many of these materials were identified with what was called "The New Age movement." They offered me a way to research this spiritual realm. My participation quickly extended beyond just reading, as I began to experiment with the various methods that were available. I had tapped into a spiritual *world* communicating with the entities that inhabit there, firmly believing that these spirits were trying to help me to achieve a higher state of *being*. All of these activities showed that indeed there was a part of me that operated in a spiritual reality. My body and spirit worked as one, opening up gateways of information that I did not even know existed. Spiritual knowledge and energy that empowered my body were suddenly at my fingertips. In addition, hidden insights about individuals (their past and future) became known. I believed that this information would help others as well as myself achieve a higher state of consciousness ultimately improving this world of ours. I still would be practicing this today, if not for God's great Mercy. In His love, He began to send His servants my way, who warned me of the dangers I had placed myself (and others) in.

Deuteronomy 18:10-12 "There shall not be found among you any one that maketh his son or his daughter to pass through the fire, or that useth divination, or an observer of times, or an enchanter, or a witch, Or a charmer, or a consulter with familiar spirits, or a wizard, or a necromancer. For all that do these things are an abomination unto the LORD: and because of these abominations the LORD thy God doth drive them out from before thee."

These *heavenly beings* that I consorted with were leading my soul toward spiritual destruction, enticing me with forbidden power and knowledge. I did not understand that my spirit was slowly drifting away from the one true Spirit of God, the Holy Spirit. I soon turned my back on this pathway to information and swore to never return.

Some of those individuals who had warned me about the New Age path I had taken were participants in a local Catholic Charismatic group. I decided to attend these meetings and see if I could learn more about my spirituality in what looked like a safe environment. For those who do not know about the charismatic movement, it is a gathering of those who want to practice the *spiritual gifts* the Bible speaks about (1 Corinthians chapter 12). Some of these gifts include words of wisdom or knowledge from God. Others are healings, prophecy, the discernment of spirits, and speaking of tongues. The individual's spirit is fully involved in this kind of activity, as their body works in conjunction with that person's spirit to manifest them. It was there I learned how to speak in tongues and to interpret them. I also experienced being 'Slain in the spirit' at one of these meetings. (Falling backward in a trancelike state when touched on the forehead, the instigator speaking a powerful word to them such as *Jesus* over and over again.) What struck me as odd was that I was utilizing the same parts of myself as I had used through the New Age methods. My body would come to a state where it would *submit* itself to a higher power. This would allow the spiritual part to express itself through the flesh. Reflecting upon this brought up some concerns. How did one know which spirit was helping or leading them? The Holy Spirit as well as any other spirit could manifest itself through our own personal spirit. It was at this time I decided to step back from this spiritual research and to focus on pure Biblical study.

I attended the various denominations in my area (Baptist, Lutheran, Jehovah's Witnesses, and Reformed to name a few) studying what each congregation believed and taught. The various doctrines that each church offered were not as cohesive as I expected them to be. One would teach a certain dogma and another would contradict that teaching. How could this happen? Didn't these churches represent the one truth from Scripture? Is God a Trinity being or not? Is Jesus God or the brother of Satan? Is there a purgatory? Can a woman be a Pastor in a congregation? How could we have so many different Biblical truths? Something was very wrong here. Fortunately, it wasn't long before the Bible showed me the answer to this important question.

John 16:13a "Howbeit when he, the Spirit of truth, is come, he will guide you into all truth..."

In order to come to all truth, God's truth, one has to be guided there by the Spirit of truth.

The Bible also teaches us that *spiritual discernment* is necessary to come to this truth.

1 Corinthians 2:12-14 "Now we have received, not the spirit of the world, but the spirit which is of God; that we might know the things that are freely given to us of God. Which things also we speak, not in the words which man's wisdom teacheth, but which the Holy Ghost teacheth; comparing spiritual things with spiritual. But the natural man receiveth not the things of the Spirit of God: for they are foolishness unto him: neither can he know them, because they are spiritually discerned."

There verses are not just teaching about the saving knowledge of Jesus Christ (believing in Him for our salvation). This also includes the deeper hidden mysteries of God's Holy Word. It is what the Bible calls the spiritual 'meat' of the Word.

1 Corinthians 3:1-2 "And I, brethren, could not speak unto you as unto spiritual, but as unto carnal, even as unto babes in Christ. I have fed you with milk, and not with meat: for hitherto ye were not able to bear it, neither yet now are ye able."

We also know this as doctrines or dogmas that come from the Word of God.

Hebrews 13:9 "Be not carried about with divers and strange doctrines. For it is a good thing that the heart be established with grace; not with meats, which have not profited them that have been occupied therein."

I asked myself, is this method of *Spiritual Revelation* being utilized in the congregations? I've been taught the basic principles to divide the Word correctly: Literally, Historically, Contextually, Grammatically, and Synthetically. So if we use this method of study, any man off the street can come to understand God's Word to a point that this person could start teaching others. In addition it is taught to look at Scripture passages utilizing symbolism and to interpret them allegorically. This form of interpretation cannot be accomplished correctly unless guided by the Spirit. The 1 Corinthians verses above tell us that it is the Holy Ghost who ultimately instructs us. By teaching the student to compare spiritual things with spiritual.

This spiritual method *trumps* all of the other interpretive methods that are taught by man.

Job 32:8 "But there is a spirit in man: and the inspiration of the Almighty giveth them understanding."

God brings understanding to man through his spirit. He communicates His *revelation* in this method. I believe this is the 'small still voice' we hear in our soul.

Because the Churches and local congregations did not allow the Holy Ghost to teach them into all truth, once they strayed from the basic Gospel message, their *advanced doctrines* began to separate them in beliefs. This eventually caused a congregation to look at another Church who taught differently and cause them to say, "They are not from God", and "Leave them, or you will perish in Hell."

1 Corinthians 12:28-29 "And God hath set some in the church, first apostles, secondarily prophets, thirdly teachers, after that miracles, then gifts of healings, helps, governments, diversities of tongues. Are all apostles? are all prophets? are all teachers? are all workers of miracles?"

Do you notice that in verse 29 the gift of teaching is listed with apostles, prophets and workers of miracles? God Himself must anoint you in order to teach others. But Churches throughout history have allowed teachers that are not anointed by the Lord to lead them.

And this has been going on for a long, long time...

There were two reasons why I wanted to write this book. The first and the most important is that I felt led by the Holy Spirit to share the information that He has graciously showed to me during my study of the Scriptures. Secondly, to warn my fellow Christians of the great danger that is coming. The Bible clearly teaches that when the spiritual roles given to the man and the woman are reversed, it is a sign to us that God will soon intervene with His creation. This has been an established pattern all throughout the Scriptures. It first manifested with Adam and Eve in the Garden. It followed the downfall of the *sons of God* right before the flood. And it brought judgment to Solomon shortly after he began to worship the gods of his wives. The New Testament is full of warnings to the churches about following the spiritual authority given to the man and woman. This *headship* created by God is for our benefit, to instruct us in our worship and prayers to Him.

Because we are instructed to be the watchman, (Ez 33:6) and if we see this destruction of God's spiritual authority, we are commanded by the Bible to send out a warning. Just as King Solomon did when God opened his understanding of this importance.

Ecclesiastes 7:25-26 "I applied mine heart to know, and to search, and to seek out wisdom, and the reason of things, and to know the wickedness of folly, even of foolishness and madness: And I find more bitter than death the woman, whose heart is snares and nets, and her hands as bands: whoso pleaseth God shall escape from her; but the sinner shall be taken by her."

Scripture teaches us that the man King Solomon was wiser than all men. (1 Kings 4:31)

He wrote most of the Proverbs, the Song of Solomon, and the book of Ecclesiastes. In chapter 7 of Ecclesiastes Solomon gives mankind a great warning about the woman. (By the way, this is not focusing on a prostitute who lures a good man into destruction as many churches teach.) He states, "whose heart is snares and nets, and her hands as bands." His description of the woman here is not at all flattering; in fact it is downright frightening. He is describing the woman's heart as a trap, and hands that can bind. What is this saying? We know that a man is given an important spiritual authority to perform in the marriage and in his home. This position requires daily dedication and sacrifices from him. The women in his life can become the biggest distraction to this, eventually drawing him away from completing this assignment. Solomon is relating from his own personal experience. Please note: this is not teaching us that a marriage is bad in God's eyes.

1 Corinthians 7:28-29 "But and if thou marry, thou hast not sinned; and if a virgin marry, she hath not sinned, Nevertheless such shall have trouble in the flesh: but I spare you. But this I say, brethren, the time is short: it remaineth, that both they that have wives be as though they had none;"

These verses teach us about the many distractions a marriage relationship can bring to your walk with God. Paul is warning us here of this *trap* Solomon writes about.

So what does "whoso pleaseth God shall escape from her" mean? Is this telling us we can get divorced? Solomon was married at the time he wrote this (under God's inspiration). No. A man of God will not be made captive of his wife, snared and bound by a wife's headship or authority. Instead, he will *rule* over his wife and guide his household in a way that pleases the Lord. The man should submit to God and to Him only. On the other hand, the wife will take those husbands who are not submitting to God, who set their own spiritual course. Solomon understood this, for he was "taken by her" (times a thousand). This warning is to all husbands, not just to those in his days. This is a battle each man must win. His wife and family are depending on him.

Jeremiah 31:22 "How long wilt thou go about, O thou backsliding daughter? for the LORD hath created a new thing in the earth, A woman shall compass a man."

As the daughters of men and those they conceived led the sons of God (right before Noah's flood), today's women and their children now set the spiritual path for mankind. The men (who became lax in their responsibilities to lead their families according to the Bible) have opened this door once again and have allowed women to be spiritually in charge. This pattern of spiritual reversal is displaying itself for the last time, in our time.

Isaiah 3:12 "As for my people, children are their oppressors, and women rule over them. O my people, they which lead thee cause thee to err, and destroy the way of thy paths."

Nahum 3:13 "Behold, thy people in the midst of thee are women: the gates of thy land shall be set wide open unto thine enemies: the fire shall devour thy bars."

Habakkuk 1:4 "Therefore the law is slacked, and judgment doth never go forth: for the wicked doth compass about the righteous; therefore wrong judgment proceedeth."

Major and minor prophets have sounded this warning to the husbands in Scripture. When we read these supporting verses, we can definitely see a warning. Women and children are an integral part of the falling away from truth. The actions displayed in the Garden of Eden continue to replay themselves over and over. The woman (or Eve) sees, desires, and takes without regard to her headship. The weaker vessel is deceived. This resulted in women needing a protector, a deliverer, or a *saviour of the body*. God places a curse on womankind in Eden to hinder the above verses from happening. And so the women's part in the falling away from Truth (God) is through deception.

1 Timothy 2:14: "And Adam was not deceived, but the woman being deceived was in the transgression."

The man (or Adam's) part was a deliberate act. He deliberately rebelled. This resulted in his being responsible for the woman's spiritual headship. But he becomes lazy; and doesn't want to fulfill the role God gives him. It is much easier to let the woman rule over them, or compass him, or have the women involved with the gates of the city. And so God has created man to *rule over her.* He has equipped man for this purpose. And He has given the man the responsibility; therefore he is held accountable.

2 Timothy 3:1-5 "This know also, that in the last days perilous times shall come. For men shall be lovers of their own selves, covetous, boasters, proud, blasphemers, disobedient to parents, unthankful, unholy, Without natural affection, trucebreakers, false accusers, incontinent, fierce, despisers of those that are good, Traitors, heady, highminded, lovers of pleasures more than lovers of God; Having a form of godliness, but denying the power thereof: from such turn away."

This is the description of our society today. Qualities like these are now promoted as something to be sought after. This behavior is not only accepted by the masses but it is also encouraged. Look at what is on television today (including advertisements), listen on the radio, search the Internet, or go see a movie. What you will find is the gospel according to the evil one. "Live for yourself." "If it feels good, do it." And don't miss the fact that today's man is portrayed either as a killing machine or a child, an idiot, in our media. Today's woman is now the authority and the role model we are to follow.

Matthew 24:37-39 "But as the days of Noe were, so shall also the coming of the Son of man be. For as in the days that were before the flood they were eating and drinking, marrying and giving in marriage, until the day that Noe entered into the ark, And knew not until the flood came, and took them all away; so shall also the coming of the Son of man be."

Spiritually, eating and drinking represent other gospels, other *blood* and *bread* that mankind is consuming. Marrying and giving in marriage represent the many other bridegrooms (and not Jesus Christ) that are accepted by the world. Most read these verses literally and understand this as everything is going on as normal in the world. But that is a superficial perspective. The spiritual state of mankind's heart and mind are now as it was in Noah's day. There is a complete lack of spiritual discernment of what is to come.

Genesis 6:5 "And GOD saw that the wickedness of man was great in the earth, and that every imagination of the thoughts of his heart was only evil continually."

Today, right before the return of Christ, both the man and the woman are so programmed to believe that it is the man who is the weaker *spiritual* vessel; and that it is perfectly natural for the woman to take on this responsibility. There is no chance of going back to God's original plan of authority or headship. This is a clear sign to us that God's plan for his creation is coming to a close. When women rule over the men (and this is achieved thru the power of Satan), there is no longer a use for mankind, it is the time for its destruction (just like in Noah's day). We are witnessing the *final signs* given us from the Bible.

Every curse that was given out by God in the Garden of Eden has been reversed. Satan no longer rules from his belly, he now stands. The woman no longer needs sorrow in childbirth (literally) or for that matter she doesn't have to have a child at all (she chooses when and if she wants one). Her desire is now to herself. Her dependency on the man for spiritual discernment is long forgotten. Her *covering* has been taken away. Today's men have also bought into this mindset. The man is an inferior being (in a spiritual sense), so they listen to their wife on spiritual matters (and follow them). They do not spiritually rule over the wife. And he no longer works the ground (Scripture), as he should, so his understanding of what to do and how to lead his family has become lost. Almost every church and congregation reflects this kind of mindset. Without the spiritual discernment given by the Holy Spirit, today's teachers and pastors propagate a style of worship that most likely matches the style practiced in the days of Noah. There are some of the faithful who still try to do it 'God's way", but they are either silenced or eventually overcome by the majority there.

1 Corinthians 11:7 "For a man indeed ought not to cover his head, forasmuch as he is the image and glory of God: but the woman is the glory of the man."

Ask yourself this very important question. Is the woman the "Glory" of the man today?